What Other People Should Know About Black People

What Other People Should Know About Black People

2nd Edition

By Sirron Kyles & Rita Houston

A Revealing Insight Into The Life Of Black Americans
During the Sixties And Seventies And Before

Table of Content

Introduction

The authors began writing this book in 1974 and completed it in 1976; the material in the book is intended to provide an intimate insight into the life of blacks and few of their achievements in the sixties and seventies in America, strictly from the point of view of the authors, who themselves are "Black" African Americans.

The content may appear offensive and controversial to anyone who may holds a self-righteous outlook about life. The material of this book has been collected through various communications and messages of older relatives, coaches, teachers and various community elders.

However, the prominent few that inspired the authors to include the content are Ms. Barbara Jordan, Mr. Hasting, Mrs. Lillian Reedy Bastine, Dr. Ira Bryant, Mr. Conrad O. Johnson, Mrs. Coach Billy Matthews, Coach Weldon Drew, President John F. Kennedy, Coach Collins Briggs, Coach Richie Guerin, Captain Van Leer Ribbink, Lt. Melton, Captain Joseph L. Coleman, Robert "Bob" Nesta Marley, "Fela" Olufela Olusegun Oludotun Ransome-Kuti, James Brown, Maya Angelou, and Muhammad Ali. Some books, magazines and journals about Blacks' history also deeply influenced the authors. The content of the researched written material is not quoted verbatim, however, some relevant points may have been paraphrased.

We have listed below the titles of some of the written material in the hope that they will serve as a reference for those readers who would like to further research the books and resources that helped in forming the author's viewpoints.

Resource List: You Forever, The Destruction Of Black Civilizations 5000 BC, The Ultimate Frontier, Roots The Saga Of An American Family, They Came Before Columbus, The Sidney Journal, Seagram's/Ebony Magazine 1976 Black History Calendar, Renegade South, History Of Unconventional Southerners, The Underground Railroad, From Slavery To Freedom and more all written about life and blacks from 1800 through 1976. We would like to reiterate that this book was written to provide an informative insight into the life of Black Americans during the Sixties and Seventies in America, for all people including African Americans.

We hope this book would surely enhance your understanding about the life of "Black" African Americans and help create a positive bond among all individuals. Thanks and enjoy the reading.

The Authors

About The Authors

Both Sirron Kyles and Rita Houston were born in Texas. Sirron Kyles is a concert promoter, music producer, entrepreneur and a business and entertainment manager. What enabled him to co-author this informative book is the experience and knowledge that that he gained from his travels which consist of three trips around the world to date, more than 20 years of constant study of people, life, political science, philosophies and other related subjects on his own.

He considers his military tours with the U.S. Navy, and his early involvement with ROTC, Houston City Honor Guard, Color Guard, Drill Team, very important that helped him establish discipline, early in his life. His quest for education besides gaining various certificates and degrees from several colleges and universities in the realm of Journalism, Communicative Broadcasting and Lithography courses equipped him with the requisite knowledge that greatly helped him in fulfilling his part in writing this informative piece of literature.

Sirron Kyles also gained the necessary foresight by playing basketball at high school, college, and professional levels along with other sports.

Sirron has always been a curious and observant individual and says, "That these traits gave him the opportunity to experience life from many different points of understanding, which he may not have been otherwise aware of." He would like to thank and acknowledge his many teachers, professors, coaches, commanding officers, employers, relatives and friends that continue to provide open minded insights into his life." He would also like to thank his parents, Joe E. Kyles and Elbenia L. Kyles, who gave him the drive to pursue higher goals.

Rita Houston gained her knowledge along similar lines as Sirron, although she did not serve in the Navy or play basketball. She did maintain a constant interest in her education and in finding a way to build unity among humanity. She thanks her late great grandmother, Mrs. Priscilla Walker who lived to be 104 years of age as well as her late grandmothers Mrs. Eliza Craft and Mrs. Rebecca Langston and a host of other friends, relatives and mentors.

Forward

"LOVE IS THE DRUG AND I NEED TO SCORE!"
NO O O O O O O ! ! NO O O O O O O ! !
DON'T TAKE IT FROM ME
PLEASE – PLEASE GIVE ME MORE
LOVE IS THE DRUG AND I NEED TO SCORE!!

You, You look like a face I can trust
I've got to have it, Oh—it's a must
The world is running out—and—
I'm scared—come on ya'll—while there's
Still time—Let's get prepared

Everyone's getting burned—they're not
Getting what they BARGAINED for
Love is the drug and I need to score!

Come along on a trip with me….
I got hooked a long time ago—I was
Turned on by two people who were
"LOVE JUNKIES" and as a result of
Their addiction, they produced other
Junkies—As each junkie grew—there
Addiction did too. Then as fate
Would have it, each young junkie tried
To Score on his own—Only to find that
He was lone in a world full of hate and
Needed a fix—But where, oh where will he
Score—The world is having a drought
Its supply of love is running out.

O cruel world let not our souls be lost—
A little sharing; a little caring; a little
Understanding—That's all it cost.
Of course the cost is higher for larger quantities—
But then, so is the HIGH—the more you invest—
The more you score!
You see—I'm a stone JUNKIE and it's
Hurting me—A world so full of hate and
Jealousy how can we expect to be free
Really, being high on love for humanity
Helps make things somewhat the way you
Want them to be and positive thoughts
Make you glow—Those who indulge seem
To know that Love is the drug you're
Looking for and they want to help you
Score.
Open your heart and let some in
Whether you lose or you win, it's a
Drug you should try again and again.
Then—Become a PUSHER—
For there is the joy—you do not
Need the street stuff the undercover
Employ.

Can't you hear my plea—Don't you see
The hatred and pain is killing me
Open up your hearts and find out what's
In store
Love is the drug and maybe we'll all score!!!

Fabu

Thoughts On Life Between Blacks And Whites In America

To our humble knowledge, there are only a few books to date that have solely been written to enlighten the Americans of all races about the life style of Black Americans and which distinctly portray their points of view as have been seen and understood by we the two ordinary Black writers who have focused only on the lives of Black Americans during the sixties and seventies. Those who are not Black and have not experienced "life" as a Black person, this book will surely provide a more explicit understanding of the struggle undergone by the male and female African decedents and their achievements while living in America during this time.

Most of the Anglo majority, White people, does not appreciate how little their understanding is about the everyday life experiences of Black people. Black people upon their arrival in America were forced to learn Whites' history; conversely, White people chose not to learn the history of Black slaves. As a result many White people not only remained ignorant about the history of Black people but focused their efforts on distorting and erasing slaves' history. Blacks were rather deliberately prevented from enacting activities from their homeland in order to maintain Whites' control and dominance over them.

England's Insurance Company, Lloyd's of London, influenced slavery in the Western Civilization. Due to the high rate of ships being sunk by

Pirates, the Company demanded that they would insure only those ships whose hulls were covered in tar. This led to the need for cheap labor to harvest rubber plants in Portugal and Haiti, (Ayiti, Quisqueya, Bohio, is the original name given by the original inhabitants who occupied the island before Christopher Columbus. The French and Spanish also named the island during their reign). Farm plantations in America's south also required cheap labor that caused the slave traders to increase slave trade.

Even now, the White people do not realize the mistake in not allowing the Black slaves learn their history, and also not educating themselves about the history of the origin of Black slaves. It is believed that the reason behind delinking of Black slaves from their past was a fear that the slaves would gain strength from the truth about their origin and their past history; this fear has ultimately created a generation who is utterly ignorant about the sentiments of Black people just because the vast majority of White people have no understanding of Black people's history.

Resultantly, many White people have least appreciation that some Black people are also prejudiced about mixing their bloodlines with White people. It is just as difficult to convince many Blacks that living in unity and ignoring the differences of color of a person's skin can only achieve World-peace. Unity and Love among all of God's children regardless of the race they may belong to, is the only way to achieve this goal; and promoting the same with full vehemence is the raison d'être for writing this book.

We earnestly hope that the book will provide a clearer insight about the American Black Populace and would help bring togetherness among all segments of American society regardless of the color of any person's skin.

Anyone reading this book would certainly belong to one or other particular race each comprising of many people. All of who would also have lots of aversions for the people of other race for any number of personal reasons. Consider those aversions and then add to them your personal dislikes. Thereafter, choose a person of different skin color/race from that of yours'; you will realize that if you add a stigma of discrimination for such a person, your feelings automatically get exaggerated and intensified with hatred. This is the prejudice and is wrong in any way you look at it. The fact is that in order to progress to the highest points of goodness, unity and love, we have to eliminate all forms of prejudices. The only thing important is who you are…regardless of the race you belong to!

All races must appreciate the merits of unity and learn to value and share the achievements of other cultures such as movies, literature and arts that have created inspiration for everyone. White people must see and appreciate the story behind movies like "Super fly", "Roots" and "Sounder" just as Black people must see and appreciate "Dr. Zhivago" "Gone with the Wind" and "Mary Poppins". The fact that each race experienced different cultures, inspirations and achievements with which we are not familiar with should actually lead us to learn from those experiences. The more each race learns from the other race and appreciates the other races' differences and achievements, the closer we will all get to a state of unity.

Black people have made many outstanding contributions in making this country what it is today. Unfortunately, it has mostly been kept secret from the public as a method of control by White society. In later chapters, you will read about many of these achievements and it is our hope you will value the many contributions black people have made towards America and the World. We will also discuss Black race classifications which is not fully understood in America…reading all of the chapters in this book will give the reader a better understanding of Black history and Black people as all topics discussed are related.

The common words being spoken around the world such as, "baldest" basketball player and "baldest" football player are just a few of many words from black dialect and have established Black origins. These and other words will also be discussed in a later chapter.

On every day, people of different races work together and remain dependent upon one another. An individual hailing from one race often holds the fates of hundreds of individuals of other race with his routine decisions on daily basis. This person could also be the person making the final decision if workers are allowed to keep their jobs. On the other hand, the employers could be White, Brown, Red, Yellow or Black. But resorting to prejudice in evaluating ones' employees is wrong and hateful but may still occur more often than not. The deciding factor for the management should always be the person's capabilities to perform the job and not the color of his skin, which unfortunately is not the norm in America today.

A Meeting Narrative That Happens in 1970
Their once was a couple that found they had no home
When they first spent time together and met in Rome
When he took her home to meet his folks…

They laughed, cussed him out, talked about him,
And said to him, surely this was a hoax…
The young lady who was upset told the young man let's go over to
My parents, we can stay with them; they knock, on door
The door opens, the mother glances at them and faints and falls flat
on the floor
The father stands with a look of shock with his mouth open and a
look of hurt
On his face that said surely nothing could be worse,
Have you lost all respect, girl they said?
Now they both feel like outcasts in a world where they are not
welcome
And are surprised they can find no place to stay at either parent's
home,
Not because they are criminals and did something wrong
It's just that one is Black and the other is White,
That in America's and other parts of the
World, society considered mixed couple wrong!

Sirron

To venture further into this relationship which one do you think is Black and which one is White; this is left to the imagination of the reader, but really should not matter, as the male or the female could easily be either. Both set of parents were wrong in their action in this narrative, and as long as there are people with this type of prejudices, self-righteousness and intolerable attitudes towards others, we will never reach total unity among all men in America or for that matter on Earth. It is a must that we strive to foster love among each other to reach higher levels of unity among all men. Review the chapter on Sex and Marriage for further information about this topic.

Born Black, White, Brown Yellow or Red, how does it matter; all evil directed towards another person is hateful, negative and wrong and therefore, should be eliminated from our thoughts and actions, and we should always be about love for our fellow men.

Little kids can play together never caring about another child's skin color. But if the same children are placed around adults who have been exposed to a prejudiced environment and let them influence these children with their hateful attitudes you would soon notice the negative changes that happen to these children that were playing together a short while ago in an environment of love.

Be proud of your race, but it has to be independent of the color of your skin. Instead it should be pride in your achievements and how you feel about unity among all races. It is wrong to prefer one skin color to another skin color as this is hateful and creates negative energy, and is as much a sin as any other sin. Make an attempt to use positive experiences that you have encountered in life, and share that knowledge to enlighten others. Make use of the positive energies you gain from sharing and it will surly lead you to a fuller, richer advancement in your own life.

There are many things about culture and advancements that White people grudgingly admit they learned from Black people as far back in history as 4500 BC. Advancements in sciences, technology, inventions and much more were learnt from the people of Northern Ethiopia, now Upper Egypt, Nubia and all of Africa. Twenty-five years ago, many White people would never have admitted that they had learned anything from Black people's history, even though Black slaves cooked meals and created many southern prescripts. They also taught the White housewives the necessary cooking skills that are in use today.

It is well known that Black people exercised a major influence on fashion in America and other fashion centers around the world for generations. Styling is a term for stylish attire as is part of black people's terminology and culture that is commonly used as part of the English language, meaning well dressed. These facts are addressed in great lengths in a later Chapter.

It is necessary that if people are to advance, everyone must strive to lift other person up, not only another Black person but anyone and everyone that needs help, every day, mentally, physical, and spiritually. Look at people through the eyes of love and not the color of their skin and only then, will you see one skin color, human.

The reasons we elected to write this book, range from shedding light on eliminating discrimination, segregation, disintegration, prejudice, and provide another tool for the better understanding of Black people. Additionally, it provides untold knowledge and history of the Black race; and of course, it strives for the spiritual advancement of all mankind.

Chapter 2

The History, Education And Contributions Of Blacks In America

The history of the arrival of Blacks in North America precedes the arrival of the Mayflower and the Declaration of Independence. Slavery began with the cycle of acquired wealth and power—you know the story—the more you have, the more you can get. Well the same type of situation existed in Africa. There were wars between tribes and the most powerful tribe conquered the weak and made them slaves and traded them to the Portuguese in exchange for artillery so that they could continue their wars of power and greed.

When the Dutch arrived in 1619 to establish colonies here, they brought with them, Dutch and Africans who could not pay their way to the New World. These Dutch and Africans signed notes stating they would work for a certain number of years to pay off their debts. Consequently, there were both black and white indentured slaves. The Indians who were already established here were taken captive and were enslaved also. The indentured slaves worked in the fields and helped to prepare the land. As the White indentured slaves began to pay off their debts, they were freed and given small sums of money to make a start.

Their freedom came with such generosity largely because they were of Dutch origin. This left only the Indians and Africans as slaves. With more of the White slaves being freed, the colonists realized they needed laborers to continue the work in their fields. The Indian slaves were not as strong as the African slaves, many of them became ill and died in the fields and others, being familiar with the territory, managed to escape. It soon became a myth that one Black slave could do the work of three Indians. The rapid death of these Indians caused the Bishop of the Indies to make a plea to the King and Queen of Spain to spare the Indians and use African slaves instead. In doing so, the entire burden of slavery fell on the shoulders of the African slave.

The Dutch were here in the New World and needed plenty of cheap labor to continue their crops. Being unable to get White laborers in large numbers, they began receiving slaves from the Portuguese, who were already skilled in slave trading. With this skill, Portugal supplied the New World with African slaves.

Okay, so there we were, a race of people in a strange land—where we were forced to live and be governed by laws of a group of people whose culture or language we didn't understand. These people already understood one another—we were the only ignorant ones who could be dominated and made to do the laboring. We did not understand what had happened—we were slaves for life-we had to learn how to remove this unwanted stigma so that we could maintain a way of life for ourselves in an acceptable, yet foreign, manner.

Much like the Vietnamese who, as a result of the Vietnam War, are being brought from their native lands to a country where they know very little about the customs, languages, cultures, values, etc., are expected to manage their lives as best as they can. What a life—many of them are too old to even try understanding the way of this new land and the young will have a difficult time for a long time. They too have been robbed of their culture—Wonder how they're going to overcome this stigma.

We had a great task before us, a long tedious battle -- one that is not half over. The progress of Blacks has depended largely on education, a positive step towards "Freedom from Ignorance". A person ignorant to certain facts should seek knowledge regarding the situation otherwise he can be easily dominated.

Before the Mayflower, many Whites had no objections towards education of Blacks, however, after its arrival, a year after the arrival of the Dutch, when the bondage of slavery was already our burden, the new settlers began to fear losing their crops because not enough laborers were available. As a result of this fear, some of the settlers began opposing the education of Blacks, stating that once the Blacks became educated, we would start thinking about freedom and trouble was sure to start. Virginia and Maryland took the lead and passed laws to further enslave Blacks. It was their feelings that all would be well if Blacks remained ignorant.

Due to our curious nature, we wanted to know what was going on around us. We wanted to understand as best we could what was happening to us as a race of people. We wanted the veil of ignorance lifted. These emotions, along with the help of Pioneers like Anthony Benezet, Prince Hall, Richard Allen, and Absolom Jones, who started schools for Blacks, initiated the battle for becoming an educated race of people. As more Blacks received education, revolts against slavery began, and with these revolts, fear spread throughout the nation. It was felt that teachers and preachers were the influences responsible for the outbreaks and, as a result, laws were passed, forbidding the gathering of Blacks unless a White man was present.

The Louisiana legislature adopted a new law requiring that the seating on railroads be assigned on the basis of color. These laws naturally made Whites feel superior to Blacks and from this law came threats to stop funding Black colleges, which was a setback, Blacks schools were already the poorest in the nation.

As Blacks showed their determination to get education, many slave owners began to feel guilty. Some of them tried to make amends. Richard Humphries willed $10,000 to the opening of a school that would teach classes on agriculture and the mechanical arts; Rev. Charles Avery provided for the establishment of Avery College in Allegheny, P.A. and Mytilda Miner started an Academy for girls in Washington, D.C. The Civil War was a developer of education rather than a hindrance. During this period, such institutions as Atlanta University (1865) Fisk University (1866) and Howard University were founded and the number of literate Blacks rose 12% between 1880 and 1890.

Much progress has been made since those times and Blacks have received education, which eventually gained us our freedom. However, segregation did not end at that point as we call the disturbance in Boston surrounding the busing of Black students to a South Boston High School in 1974; and during his presidential campaign, ex-President Nixon stated that he would oppose busing to achieve voluntary racial balance. This would, if it were possible, have been fine, that way people could attend the school of their choice.

Blacks are not concerned with the fact that the school is all White or that we will be associated with Whites; what we are concerned about is a form of education which is being conducted in certain schools and is different in quality and more extended in detail than what is being offered on the same level in a particular social environment. It is the desire for knowledge that makes man seek other learning tiers. For this reason we want the opportunity to acquire all available information, which would enable us to make better living for ourselves.

The answer is not necessarily accomplished through attending predominately White schools, however, it may be in system where in the knowledge is provided.

The value of education is emphasized in Black families as a means of elevating oneself beyond the accomplishments of the generations before him. With the requirements for maintaining a place in the system that is continuously changing and becoming ever more demanding—and to meet those demands one must be equipped with the educational levels in existence during his time.

Many Blacks are unable to obtain an education today for basically the same reason that existed in the early 1960's—FINANCE. Financing plays a major role in obtaining higher education. Sure, there are a great many programs through which Blacks can secure financing for education, however, many of them have such stipulations as loans being granted to students whose families are in a certain income bracket, a bracket wherein it is almost impossible to survive, or in some instances the available funds are not publicized in a manner where it would reach those who need them most.

Take the man whose primary concern is being able to provide his family with the basic necessities of life (Food, Clothing and Shelter) so that they may prosper and be able to cope with their environment. At the end of a day wherein he has dealt with the system and the mental frustrations involved therein, his mind is usually cluttered with thoughts of as to how he will cope with tomorrow; therefore, he cannot fully access the guidance needed nor can he take the necessary time to see that the information and opportunities are being made readily available. More often than not, he is unaware of what programs are available to his family.

There are those who are fortunate enough to have the type of job, which leaves their minds free so that they can lend the helping hand necessary to guide a child in the right direction towards securing an education so that they are better able to aid in being the backbone of tomorrow's nation. We must be assured that if opportunity knocks, our youth are in the right place at the right time, as we rely largely on their self-motivation.

In many families where the income is low, the decision of which child to educate has to be made. In most instances, it was the female who got the education. The male, once reached employment age, or sooner than that, had to take the responsibility of helping and supporting his family, or at least him. This happened because it was the feeling that the men could easily make a substantial living without the education or perhaps he would join a branch of the Armed Forces. Also, due to the physical and mental make up of women, they could not perform the type of jobs that a man could perform in order to support themselves.

Many of these men acquired skills after high school and supported themselves by what is called "common labor". Some became construction workers, factory workers, seamen, carpenters, barbers, shoe repairmen, etc., and made good livings for their families. We are proud of their accomplishments no matter how large or small they may seem because Black men have had to learn early in life how to survive—the name of the game. Recent years, however, have shown an increase in the number of Black men getting college educations.

Take your big industries for example, they survey and recruit minority high schools for the best students in a particular field, pay for their education and give them jobs. Years later, you find those same students in those same level jobs. To the public, this gesture makes the industry look very big. "They are helping the minorities". Look closer, whom, have they really helped? The industry in the long run receives the biggest reward, they keep their government contracts, get a tax break for the monies spent to educate these students and get good workers for less money.

Yes, the student has a job he may not have gotten otherwise, but of what real value is it if his chances for advancement are nil? His future begins and ends at the dead end job. The student has a choice to either remain locked in this position, continue his education (which usually creates some problem) or leave the job and seek other employment.

If he chooses the latter, as is the case in most instances, he loses his job seniority, his benefits and sometimes takes a reduction in pay. Recognizing the fact that obtaining an education is only one step towards achieving equality—we wonder, with the ever increasing demands being placed on achievement, if education is not just another form of elimination—of course, giving credit to the fact that some system must be used as more and more people are becoming educationally qualified. Look at the present situation, check it out, and judge for yourself.

The struggle towards getting an education soon began to show rewards after the Civil War. As we became more educated, our curiosity grew. Before long, we had amongst us men who were later called scientists and inventors. Perhaps the greatest injustice meted out to these inventors and scientists is the fact that many of them and their contributions have been buried in White American history.

Ray Charles, a famous Black recording artist, describes the plights of the unknown Black contributors in his country & western version of "Look What They Done To My Song, Ma".

> …The only thing I could half
> Right, now it's turning out all wrong
> ….Look what they done to my brain-
> They picked it like a chicken bone now
> I'm about to get insane…Look what
> They done to my song…

All because they didn't feel that Blacks were intelligent enough to be taken seriously about their inventions and other scientific matters. This song depicts what has happened to many Black inventors and scientists who, for some reasons beyond their control, were not recognized. Norbert Rillieuz (the natural song of a slave owner who chose to make him free) could have appreciated this song—he submitted a plan for a sewage disposal system to the city of New Orleans, which was rejected, and a few years later, a plan similar to his was accepted.

A great many contributions to the fields of entertainment, athletics and the liberal arts were made by familiar names as Joe Louis, Jesse Owens, Bessie Smith, Ira Aldridge, Phyllis Wheatley, Billie Holiday, Louis Armstrong, etc.—the list could go on and on. However, what's to be said on behalf of the many unknown who were never able to enter a world where their abilities and desire to know would have been recognized? Many of these men were successful and in doing so had more than their share of frustration in trying to research and perfect these projects—they were either financially unable or afraid of what might happen to a "Smart Nigger".

Some of the inventions that Blacks got little or no national recognition for are: The Lubricating Cup (a mechanism which permitted the flow of oil to gears and other parts of the engine of trains, eliminated the need to stop the operation of a train for service) by Elijah McCoy;

The Dynamotor (an apparatus that made a single unit of the motor and generator of street cars which kept them from catching fire while moving); The Trolley (a device which kept the street cars from jumping track); The Multiplex Telegraph (enabled a railroad dispatcher to inform trains of the exact position of other trains so that they could avoid collisions) and an Air Brake system for street cars and subways are inventions of Granville T. Woods; The Lasting Machine (a machine that sewed the top of a shoe to the inner sole) by Jan Matzeliger (where would the shoe industry Be Today Without This Invention);

The Water Closets For Trains Was Invented By Lewis Latimer, the Fire Safety Hood, was invented By Garrett A. Morgan, this invention kept firemen from being overcome by smoke fumes and as poison gas became acceptable as a weapon, various armies and policemen used the Hood. Seeing the need to make the streets safe for pedestrians and motor vehicles, Morgan also invented the first Automatically Timed Traffic Light. Granville T. Woods also invented a type of telephone that he sold to the Bell Telephone Company because he could not finance the project himself. Such was the case for many inventors. Those who were able to secure financial backers did so at the price of part ownership of the invention.

It is speculated that many of these contributions went unrecognized because the inventors and scientists lacked communication with other inventors and scientists, therefore, they were unable to exchange knowledge and many of the inventors were slaves and a slave was considered the personal possession of his master, likewise his invention also became the possession of his master. Practical and logical reasoning shows that these inventions were the results of slaves, as it was they who performed the actual labor and were seeking ways to make their chores less burdensome and more efficient. Because they sought easier ways to accomplish their chores, Blacks were often referred to as being shiftless and lazy.

Believing this and being ridiculed for the very idea of unheard of objects and discoveries, many of them abandoned their projects. As a result, they were not aware of what they had accomplished and much of the renowned credit for similar inventions went to those who were wealthy, titled and privileged. History will show that a great many of the inventions for which the wealthy got credit were initiated by slaves and perfected by those with the capital to back them.

Our curious nature combined with the fact that we had to "make do" with what was available and were able to make the best of it are probably the reasons most Whites feared and opposed educating Blacks. The first American made clock was the result of the curiosity of Benjamin Banneker, a descendant of African slaves, who after seeing a pocket watch, made a clock entirely from wood. Because they were not financially able to perfect these inventions, many heard their works referred to by such mockery as being "Nigger

Rigged", which in itself was a horrible blow. As much of the wealth of the New World came from the hard labor of Blacks who never received a paycheck until some 250 years—even then the pay was nominal. Scientists such as Dr. Charles Drew, Dr. Daniel Williams and George Washington Carver were great contributors to the scientific developments of Blacks and they underwent many of the same financial and discriminatory frustrations as the inventors of their eras.

At a time when all farmers were growing peanuts and had no available market for them, the farmers found themselves in trouble. George Washington Carver, who had done a great deal of research on peanuts, sweet potatoes, pecans and soybeans, was invited by the United Peanut Association of America to attend their meeting in Montgomery to offer advice and tell of his discoveries.

Upon arriving at the hotel, he was confronted by a doorman who refused him admittance. After being convinced that Carver was in fact to attend the meeting, the doorman led him to the meeting room by way of the "back door" and "freight elevator". Imagine the humiliation and bitterness this man of considerable knowledge must have endured. Other humiliations of this nature did not stop his research. His discoveries from the peanut included a form of synthetic rubber, hand & face creams, and various oils, inks, etc.

Dr. Daniel Williams performed open heart surgery in 1893 on a black man who had been involved in a bar fight and the only way to save his life was to open the chest and find what was causing the internal bleeding. Realizing that in doing so, the man could die and he would be banned from practicing medicine if he failed, Dr. Williams felt the need to try and save a life. Dr. Williams experienced many discriminatory practices when he became a surgeon, as many of the hospitals would not admit Blacks. This caused him to carry out most of his surgeries in his office or at the home of the patient.

Dr. Charles Drew really had a rough "row to hoe". He was the result of crossbreeding, which gave him white-like features. There were some who tried to persuade him to "pass" for White, in hopes of making his missions easier and others who thought he should become a professional athlete rather than face the hardships of being a black doctor. Dr. Drew ignored both suggestions and became a great credit to his people. As he began his research for methods of storing blood plasma for long periods of time and as he perfected it, he encountered problems with the Military and the Red Cross, the administrating agency for the National Blood Bank Program which was initiated in 1941, and established policies that blood taken from Black soldiers be given only to other Black soldiers—they believed such myths that if a White soldier received the blood of a Black soldier, he would turn black or have black offspring.

How fatuous! In 1950, Dr. Drew was injured in an automobile accident wherein he suffered internal and external wounds. Upon arrival at the nearest hospital, which happened to be all white, he was refused admittance. At a hospital where Blacks were admitted he was given plasma, but by that time, it was too late—he died.

How fortunate are we as a race of people that these men were too big to let such obstacles interfere with their contributions—contributions that improved the intellectual abilities of Blacks.

In more recent years, programs through which Blacks are supposedly able to secure financing for businesses, research. Etc., have become available. However, these programs for the most part are full of technical requirements, long waiting periods and under certain programs, if a loan request is rejected, the application cannot be resubmitted to the same organization ever. These programs were initiated to lend a helping hand to aspiring Blacks, yet if it appears that one will do well or more than what the system will tolerate, then the loan can be rejected for income projections being "too optimistic"!

It is sad to note that after more than 200 years, in spite of the many, many accomplishments and the progress made by Blacks, the lack of financing for self-motivated projects is still a barrier the Black man has not been able to break—wonder why? Could it be that the system still regards him as inferior and feels threatened by his very existence? It appears that the only major change, which has occurred, is in the methods used to keep the majority of Blacks from becoming self-sufficient—another reason hypertension is an ailment more commonly found in Blacks.

Classification Of Native Blacks Of America

This chapter is about finding the unique origins of Black people in America. Today the politically correct term is African American and the most commonly used term is Black. The classification of Black people, especially in America, has been altered many a times as a result of slavery, although other countries have also gone through some identity reclassifications for black people. In America it is generally known that slaves birth names, tribes and origins were erased and forbidden to be spoke about by their slave owners. While most of the slaves were given names by their owners, some also chose to use names from what they had learned about their tribes. Yet others used names they learnt from their elder slave ancestors to gain respect among rest of the slaves for holding on to there past. Many sought out new identities after escaping through the Underground Railroad to the North.

There are five known classifications of black people that have been used over the past few centuries. They are Negro, Nigger, Colored, African American and Black. The first three were names created by white southern slave owners; the last two are names that blacks selected to define themselves. This chapter will go in to detail to describe and define what each name means to Black people as well as others.

Negro—members of the Black race distinguished according to physical features but without regard to language or culture from members of other races that have African ancestry. "Negro" is the name that the White slave owners first gave to their slaves to identify them during slave trading. Since that time, Blacks names have changed several times, still those that refer to their race as many Negros, still have not found out who they are, not even at the time of writing this book. Most Black people have yet to define the true definition of what the word "Negro" actually means; the definition in Spanish means Black. The belief of some Blacks who define the meaning as such "true Americans" with high patriotic ideals but inferior to the White race.

There are Black people who have for years used the name Negro and believe themselves as Black people inferior to White people; and willingly, because of brainwashing, accept the term, Negro**; these** Blacks generally belong to the older generations, as if they are locked in a time warp, they have not sought justification of higher wages, wages owed and equal rights because in their minds they are still Negros, and without guts to seek their own identity. They consciously do not realize the demeaning nature of the name, and as long as they believe they are Negros, they never will. You can recognize Black people who considered themselves Negros today simply by observing how they react negatively to being called "Black".

Nigger—Another classification created for slaves by white slave owners in America. This name was meant, from its origin, to be offensive and demeaning, a slur of the word Negro. The meaning slave owners gave to it generally related to anyone whom they felt it applied. During the slave era of the U.S., any slave who did not perform his or her work up to the standards of their slave masters, was called, lazy, shiftless, ignorant, trifling, good for nothing, and "Nigger" as a way to further demean him/her.

History says southern White slave owners that spoke with a southern drawl first brought this word into existence, simply by not being able to correctly pronounce the word Negro when referring to more than one.

As a result they pronounced it Neg-gra and for more than one, they created the word niggers. The word is still used today by a great number of people who use the word Nigger for demeaning purposes, and in a variety of social circumstances it is used by some to relate anyone that is Black, White, Brown, Yellow are Red. The people that tend to use the word as casual slang are normally in music or as gang lingo and many other social settings; to them it has a different meaning when it is used, even though it is a derogatory word in any use. The word has become normal to use by many people who consider the word a badge of unity even when they are called Nigger in public without regard to others around them that consider the word an insult.

Colored—This classification was the first classification; many Black people were comfortable being so classified. The Webster's Dictionary defines the word "Colored" as African that is mixed. During the days of slavery Colored was one of the many names used for the offspring of the White slaves owners and other mixed races. There were other names such as Mixed Breed, Mullato, and Half-Breed etc., but most Black people favored the name Colored, basically because it made more sense to them. They became aware of the many that were mixed amongst them either with White, Brown, Red or Yellow that also used the term "Colored", when referring to their offspring.

Those that considered themselves Colored were mixed with white or other races and appeared to give the impression that they were better than Black people who were not mixed. This feeling of superiority went on and still continues in America. Today, it is the general conception that others, than their darker skinned counterparts, treat light skinned Blacks differently. This perception surfaced during the periods of slavery, and persists even today. It, however, created, for those who considered themselves Colored, an illusion that they had a chance to move up in status, warranted or not.

Those who labeled themselves as colored expected that due to their lighter complexion they could win acceptance of whites. A startling fact was soon to dawn upon this segment of Black people that while sometimes they were able to obtain a token respect from White people, they received little or no respect from darker skinned Blacks, who believed lighter skinned Blacks thought they were better than them. Their conception was that they were attempting to imitate White people.

It, on the other hand, was not very uncommon to observe the earlier Colored Blacks getting their hair straightened known as conked, processed, or pressed; and they were also seen practicing their speech dialect to emphasize the way northern White people spoke. They also dressed, in public, more conservatively to blend with White people. It, therefore, is a fact that everything that was done by the people who classified themselves as colored pointed towards mimicking the White behavior. Even in the sixties and seventies, those who considered themselves colored, were subjected to insults if they were to be labeled as, or called Black or African-American. These are the next two classifications discussed in this chapter.

African-American—This term is applied to the group of people born in America and having an African lineage. The term was originated during the late fifties and early sixties; and ultimately got a definition in the seventies. It is the only classification other than "Black" that provides a true identity and due respect to them. After years of quest in search of their identity, having been lost after getting uprooted from their homeland as slaves, "African- American" is a term that most Black people can associate with. After acquiring the term African-American for them and identifying themselves as such, many White people felt irritated; and considered them to be raciest and militant niggers. Most of them, especially the southerners, thought they needed to be taught a lesson, as they were getting too big for their britches.

With the usage of the term African-American came a corresponding change in the Black people as regards their dress, attitude and sense of pride. The majority of Black people ceased to consider it inferior to White people. This era also introduced the Natural and Afro hairstyles, African fashion style clothing, art, music and literature and a greater respect for other Black people. An extensive study of history and culture of the race was also undertaken during the same period, something that many had little interest or opportunities before and had caused scanty knowledge about their history and heritage.

Prohibited to learn anything involving their former homeland and history; and conversely, forced to study the history of White people by their owners, the slaves, over time, forgot their true identity and culture. During the awakening period that had begun in the fifties, African-Americans who, in the past, had feared White people overcame that fear and began to raise their voices in a variety of ways. Some paid with their lives in violence for equal rights as human beings. African-Americans gradually began to be recognized for demonstrating pride in their ancestry and their strength.

It needs to be kept in mind that the Blacks who later chose to use the term and considered themselves African-American had generally felt some disdain and hatred towards White people, and naturally so, for the memory of the many wrongs and mistreatment of the generations of their grandparents. It, however, is something that the people have had to slowly over come that disdain as time went by.

Black—Now at the peak of their awaking, the Black people have found solace in being classified as Black. It is a term, which has universally been accepted for identifying the Black race. Black Identity is very important and it is how Black people see themselves and relate to who they are. It is now same as the majority of White people relate to the term White as who they are in the box they check on Government forms. Currently, a box marked as Black has been added on such forms for the Black people to relate to who they are and check. So far the word Negro or colored has been removed on most Government forms, but some States, mostly the Southern States, still retain the word Colored and Negro, mainly to create confusion among Black people.

A Black person while relating to the term Black must realize that it is not just about color of his skin, instead it is an idea of mind, an identity of respect and knowledge of the history and heritage of the race to which he belongs. Just thirty years ago to call a Black person Black would more often than not result in a verbal or fist fight. This is simply the hangover effect of being brain washed and taught that White was right and good and Black was bad, evil and wrong. Still today some older Black people continue to relate to the color negatively by remembering how the words were used by whites for so long and accepted that the word Black does not mean any of those words, they will not like to be known as Black.

This revolutionary change in the black community has not only occurred in the political, social and economic institutions; but more importantly has occurred in the minds of Black people who acknowledge that they are Black as an identity. These internal changes have brought about an enhanced self-awareness, a newfound appreciation of "Blackness" and restructuring of the image of Black. That same mood which is echoing the essential tragedy and triumph of the Black experience in America brought on a blossoming of Black arts, a great interest in Black studies, inventions, and in general a value that has grown and continues to grow in the Black Community.

The truth is that there is only one color that should really matter in all men's minds and that is a perfect blending of all races skin colors and minds that would end up as the color beige. If you could take all of the colors that relate to races, White, Black, Red, Brown, Yellow, etc. and inter-mix them mentally and physically, then all minds would broaden to the point that the color of skin would not matter.

Keep God in mind to create unity, always remembering that it is all about Love not Hate and there really is not a difference in loving all men as one, just as all are loved by God, regardless of the color of their skin.

The Root Of Race Classification & Racism

The root of Race Classification and Racism is Fear; Racism, came to the forefront against people with African heritage thousands of years ago, when it was recognized that features of a race made a difference when it came to the offspring of mixed race couples, as the children will have features of the dominant African Heritage parent.

White Americans are both genetically weaker and less diverse than their Black compatriots, a Cornell University-led study finds, Fox News Reports. http://www.foxnews.com/story/2008/02/22/whites-genetically-weaker-than-blacks-study-finds.html

Analyzing the genetic makeup of 20 Americans of European ancestry and 15 African-Americans, researchers found that the Whites showed much less variation among 10,000 tested genes than did the Blacks, which was expected. They also found that Europeans had many more possibly harmful mutations than did African, which they said was a surprise.

"We tend to think of European populations as quite large, we did not expect to see a significant difference in the distribution of neutral and deleterious variation between the two populations," said senior co-author Carlos Bustamante, an assistant professor of biological statistics and computational biology at Cornell. White Europeans make up 16% of the worlds population, compared to 25% thirties years ago.

It's been known for years that all non-Africans are descended from a small group, perhaps only a few dozen individuals, who left the African continent between 50,000 and 100,000 years ago. But the Cornell study, that Europeans went through a second "population bottleneck," probably about 30,000 years ago, when the ancestral population was again reduced to relatively few in number.

The doubly diluted genetic diversity has allowed "bad" mutations to build up in the European population; something that the more genetically varied African population has had more success in weeding out. "What we may be seeing is a 'population genetic echo' of the founding of Europe," said Bustamante. Simply put, White Europeans have difficulty in breeding with some one they are not related too.

The doubly diluted genetic diversity has allowed "bad" mutations to build up in the European population; something that the more genetically varied African population has had more success in weeding out. The Root cause of White Europeans Racism towards African people of color is their own fear of extinction, through no fault of any other race, but the few whose genetics White Europeans share, Just Saying.

Dialect And Mannerisms

"I done told you". "He'd be back". "Sometime Mama be cookin' she burn her hand". "You don't get no more". "Hey, man, you really doin' it".

It is easy to note that the speakers of the above phrases are of Black origin. Why is it so recognizable—it could be that according to the guidelines of Standard English, it is improper to speak this way and (according to myths we all know) Blacks don't use "Good English" (meaning Standard English); it could be jive talk or it could be that distinct characteristics of Black English are present? Black English—the basic dialect of Blacks—is a form of communication with which we readily get identified.

Many (Blacks as well as Whites) have ignored or forgotten the fact that Blacks "had" a separate language. For a long time, this country has tried to deny them their African heritage, which is the primary reason for the misunderstandings surrounding the speech of Black Americans.

Take an average two or three years old child who is beginning to talk, ask him to say the word "three" and chances are he'll say something that sounds like "free"; tell him to say "gum" and he'll probably say "dum". Take requisite time and show him the movements of the mouth and lips and he'll say the words correctly. The same principal needs to be applied for learning words of a foreign language. What happens to the person who is not taught the correct (by the standards of the language in question) way to say a word—he will come as close to the pronunciation as is possible for him on his own. We had this problem!

During the periods of early Portugal & British slave trade with the New World, the slave traders practiced language-mixing aboard ships housing captives from many different tribes speaking as many different languages. Knowing that their captives could object to slavery, language mixing was resorted to, to discourage escape attempts by them. This strategy ensured little understanding among their captives/slaves and made the slave traders feel safer.

After arrival in the New World, further language mixing occurred and with the different practices on different plantations, many abandoned their native languages and were forced to learn another one so that they could communicate with their peer groups. Many of the slaves were already speaking Portuguese Pidgin that they had learned in the slave factories on the West Coast of Africa; however, Pidgin English (a form of communication which has no set or formal rules) became a common bond between slaves. Many slaves knew and used two or more of these varieties and began to teach them to each other. The separation of slaves as house servants and field workers created two language groups; the house servants learned the Standard English of their masters and the field servants spoke a form of Plantation Creole. The widespread use of West African Pidgin English mixed with Plantation Creole gave birth to a form of Black English.

Since a person's surrounding determines and dictates his dialect, the migration of Blacks from the south to other parts of the country brought about variations of Black English. A Black from the North can easily relate to the meaning of statements like "He be serious" coming from a Black of any other part of the country. Blacks raised in an environment where they have few or no Black associates or Whites who spend a considerable amount of time with Blacks will naturally take on the ways of their peers.

Many Southern Whites picked up the dialect from their Black playmates, nannies, Uncle Charlie's, etc. As we abandoned our native languages along with Pidgin English, many of us began learning Standard English; therefore, Black children grew up learning not the language of our ancestors, but code switching, a mixture of Black English and Standard English.

This created a problem for the children who must learn Standard English and its different rules and grammar and are taught by teachers who don't understand the Black English the students speak and hear at home. This accounts for the lower scores made by Blacks on tests which are standardized to white cultural patterns—robbed of our African Cultural Patterns amounts to cooking in someone else's kitchen. Considering this handicap, along with many others, it is not a mean achievement for us to have mastered Standard American English as best as we could. The realization that we "had" our own language with its own rules disproves the myths that the dialect of Blacks is due to laziness, carelessness or from having "thick lips". Since each language has its own set of rules and character that could be markedly different from those of the other languages, one linguistic group may un-thoughtfully foster animosity towards the other linguistic group.

A distinguishable characteristic of the Black English is its usage of the verb. The dropping of the "g" if the main verb ends with "ing" (He goin' tomorrow) does not require a form of "to be" before the main verb. The verb "be" expresses action that is continuous or occurs at intervals rather than an expression of action from the time of its occurrence (he be walking the beat). "Done" is used before the main verb in the same respect as the axillary have (I done told you before). The third person singular present tense does not require "s" (She do rather than She does).

"Been" and "Done" are usually put together when negation occurs. In Black English only one verb in a sentence needs to be marked in tense although more than one may be used. "Is" is used to either be emphatic or as a question maker (The teacher is nice! Is the teacher nice?). The negative structure as well as the double negative structure is a result of Plantation Creole mixed with Pidgin English.

Many a teacher would fail worse than those students they find so awkward if tested on the structure, meaning, etc. of Black English. Many words and phrases have been contributed to Standard American English by Blacks, for example the word "Pickaninny" is a Portuguese word many African slaves heard during the Portugal slave trade in reference to "a child slave". We in turn referred to each child as a pickaninny and the Whites, wanting to communicate with us in our language, picked up the word to refer to "all black children".

"Cat" is a West African word for person; "Uh huh" & "Uh uh" are West African Words for yes and no; "hipcat" and "hipicat", later turned to "Hepcat" by the distorted translation of Whites, is a Wolof term which means a man who is aware or has his eyes open. Other terms are:

"Long time no see, Bo, bogus, boogie, chick, bug, bamboula, bad eye, he with it, No can do, jazz, okra, goober, bad mouth, chigger/jigger, dig, dirt, jamboree, jelly-roll, humbug, jitter, okay, bukra/buckaroo, juke, tote, hoodoo/voodoo, hanjo, ofay, zombie, pin, and rooty-toot".

Evidence that characteristics of the old form of Black English, in a more acceptable manner, is still around and is presented through poets like Nikki Giovanni, Langston Hughes, Gil Scott and other artists as an expression of black unity, showing pride in the expressive power of our language. Well-known recording groups are using forms of code switching in the lyrics of their songs.

One such group, Rufus, in their song "Stop on by", used the word "that" to mean "who". In a recent TV Variety Show, a well-known Black Entertainer used another form of code switching in his closing remarks, "We'll be coming back atcha". Recently, I overheard a conversation between two people wherein the speaker, explaining an incident, used the phrase, "Don't be for the glass…" Recent years show that much of the colloquialism considered the "in thing to say" in a given situation is initiated by Blacks, for instance: "rappin", "coppin' a plea", "shuckin' & jivin'", "playing the dozens", "right on", "honky", "do ya thang", "square business", "that's cold" and use of "bad" to mean "good".

As we become more aware of our heritage, it is good to note that many are making efforts towards restoring to our native languages and with colleges offering classes in various African languages, it won't be long before our identity, as a race of people, will be recognized in our language as well as other facets.

Rhythm, harmony and melody are the basis of Black mannerisms and like dialects; mannerisms are geographically and socially distributed. Notice the gutsiness in the way we move, talk, laugh, etc. Being full of emotions and very expressive, many of us do roll our eyes and perform dances when we laugh. There are ways of being emphatic about what we do. We relate to situations straight from the heart—we feel what we do and tell it like it is. In order to do so, we use gestures, which help convey how we really feel about a given situation.

Some of the gestures used today are the results of mixing distinct African Cultures with slavery and the American society. The problem in dealing with these mannerisms is that because they are used more widely by "regulars", members of other ethnic groups believe them to be militant and are used in defiance of the American Culture when, in fact, they are traditions of African Culture and are used to express unity and pride.

One thing is certain to a Black man rhythm are a natural characteristic. In dancing, each part of the body moves separately from the other, yet it happens simultaneously. These movements are controlled by the songs messages.

When you feel music and can relate to the message, your emotions will naturally cause you to move like you feel. Your arms, feet, hips, knees, fingers, etc. seem to have a mind of their own. The uniqueness in the walk of Blacks is the all over rhythm and backward and forward motion of the shoulders, which sway naturally. In the graceful stride, one foot is placed directly in front of the other with the heel touching first. The leg drops loosely. The Black female has a certain back and forth hip swinging motion with her walk.

To indicate agreement and approval or to pay a compliment, we use the gestural expression of "giving skin" (palm to palm contact of back or hand to palm). The straightforward and upward movement of the arm exposing the palm is traditional African culture for hello and goodbye and is unlike the waving motion of the Anglo American Society. The Black Power handshake is used to express togetherness, strength, unity and friendship. The fundamentals of the handshakes are the mutual encircling of the thumb and the grasping of each other's hand with bended fingers; the mutual grasping of wrists and hands and the placing of the hand on the shoulder of a friend with a small amount of pressure applied. Also indicative of the pride, unity and respect we feel are the "Black Power Sign" (the raising of the arm and making a fist), the Afro, natural and corn row hairstyles.

Blacks on a whole have been regarded as happy-go-lucky, flashy and musical people because of our nonchalant attitudes, flashy cars and clothes. This was due to the myth that we never disagreed with anything the white may have said or did—he was always right. This myth brings to mind a childhood jingle we used to recite at play, "if you're white, you're right if you're black or brown, you better get out of town" which is indicative of how brainwashed we were about being Black.

By appearing happy-go-lucky, many of us were able to achieve what we wanted because very little attention was paid to the grinning, foot shuffling Black, which ironically worked to our advantage, as an "Uncle Tom" was not suspected of trying to better his conditions.

Flashy cars and clothes were status symbols for many Blacks. Very few were fortunate enough to own cars and when we were financially able to secure one, it was usually flashy in color and if possible the make was Cadillac. Being second financially to Whites and unable to acquire cars like the Mercedes, Porsche, etc., to the financially successful Black the Cadillac was the top of the ladder.

It is safe to assume that the natural mannerisms of Blacks are inherited. These gestures are instilled in us and were passed on from our ancestors. Expressing ourselves in a certain fashion is not something we were trained to do—it just happens!

Chapter 5

Sex And Marriage

Interracial sex and marriages have been historically controversial issues for races from their first known records. Monarchs insisted that in order to keep the bloodline as pure as possible, marriage was to be between other Monarchs of the same clan. And, in the event of non-availability of another royal of the same race and blood line, marriage was even allowed within a family, under exceptional circumstances, to ensure the purity of would-be offspring.

In America slavery brought about a broad range of problems to the forefront for White people especially the slave owners, when it related to the offspring of Black people, whom they considered slaves property without any rights. In many cases they were not even allowed to marry and have sex with another slave, which was prohibited. If discovered they split the family, child, man and woman and sold them to another slave owner. This meant the slave owners, kept their stock fresh, and in reality helped them in having sex with any slave they chose to have sex with.

As slaves, Black women, just like Black men had no rights when it came to what their slave owners could do to them. They were subject to all forms of injustices including rape that were common even at very tender age by their slave masters. Male slave owners saw Black woman as an exotic full-bodied sexual tool that aroused and excited them unlike many of their wives who by nature were no more than childbearing bed partners and companions. Most of them were portrayed as prudish with self-righteous morals and religious cultural hang-ups and who also lacked excitement of expressions unlike their slave Black women counterparts, due to the difference in upbringing, environment and morals.

Children that were born out of rapes and fornication by male and female slave masters introduced a new generation of Black people in America. These crossed-bred children out of Black and White parents would be called "Colored". As time went on, these children favorites of the slave masters were sent to work in the slave owners' main houses and classified as house Niggers by slave masters because of their lighter skin color. Not all of these children were born from female slaves as the wives of the slave masters also used male slaves for sex without the knowledge of their husbands. Resultantly, when they got pregnant and bore children, much to the disgust and shock of their husbands who would then either kill them or secretly sell them off to other slave owners.

After the abolishment of slavery, Black people were legally allowed to marry within their race that would bring back family unity. They were thus very grateful as marriage was denied to them throughout slavery. Still for decades black married couples had to struggle through tough times barley making both ends meet and some also had to become indenture servants by working for their former slave owners to pay of the price of the land they lived on, but saw family unity in doing so, as the only way they could survive as a family.

These struggles are also the reason that so many families were left as single parents families. Many husbands often left to find work in other towns, in hopes of making money for their families, yet many of them never returned and on occasions the female jilted with other men, due to the stress of family life, leaving everything behind including their children.

The truth is that the slavery was the real issue that created much of the split between Black families then and today, due entirely to the financial stresses created by years of oppression they had suffered without payment for their services.

Marriages in the Black race usually end now days not from divorce, but in separation. The reasons are basically the same that are encountered by most marriages in any race, and that are poor financial situations and sexual incompatibilities etc. The financial needs are usually the basis behind why a lot of blacks separate and never get a divorce, as they could not afford to do so.

Other races have for centuries, considered black men and women as hot-blooded and sexually appealing. The Black males were considered to be physically more athletic and stronger than males of other races and that was the real reason slavers perused them for use as slave workers. Black female usually have full figure, large breasts, full hips and a round (not flat) booty. From their tribal roots, sex has always assumed an active and vital role in the lives of the Black people; for them energy and eroticism are just as important as food, music and religion.

This sexuality has not been lost on the younger generation of Blacks, which has shown more openness and freedom than their older generation by publicly expressing their sexuality and which has led to a willingness to seek and experience companionship and sexual relations with other races. The erotic allure of having sex with Black females and males by men and women of various races around the world especially the Whites have always been a wondering fantasy that although not fully accepted is more obvious in today's society.

Born from the rhythms of Africa, Black males and females learned early to move and rotate their bodies to the rhythm of their mates when having intercourse. By coinciding these movements with their partners with back and forth thrusting motion they learned that it increases their enjoyment and a sense of unity with their mate and generally tend to create affectionate passion when and while they are involved with sex, which also increases in their minds the sense of loyalty for each other.

All females including Black women look for compatibility as they select and chose companions. A little known fact about Black people is that they were somewhat prejudiced towards members of other races and many of them chose not to pursue relationships with other races. But as times have changed Blacks' friends come in all colors and races and if they find some particular person of another race they are compatible with, they do share their feelings the same way as other races. Some Black women believe that white men are uninteresting, somewhat square (a bore), but others judge any man on how that man makes them feel when they are around them.

Most Black females from lack of experience and knowledge except what they have read about White men feel that White men are physically unable to handle their physical sexual desires and still hold grudges deep down for how slave owners treated their ancestors.

Oral sex is a taboo for the majority of Black people, more so for black men than Black women, as the women are believed to have provided oral sex for men as means to sexually satisfy their mates, or to keep from getting pregnant and during menstruation or forced to perform the act by men.

Nevertheless, Black women have been open to providing oral sex and appear to be more comfortable with oral sex than Black men. Conversely, Black men consider it something dirty what the white men do because of White men's genitals shortcomings and the belief that women's genitals are not clean because of menstruation.

But as quite as it's kept many Black men have and do participate in providing oral sex to please their partners. But they usually keep what they do behind closed doors because of the fear that if known by friends they provided oral sex to a woman; they would be heckled and ridiculed by them for eating "Pussy".

History and Art have depicted Black men as being well endowed, with large penises and this has been a blessing for them as many women around the world have secretly and openly desired having sex with Black men due to this belief, but it has also been a curse as when they were enslaved and forced to be servants, the slavers generally had them castrated to keep them from having sex with their females. Research studies have proven that the males from the continent of Africa generally have larger bodies which may have something to do with the size of their penises, but not all black men have larger penises, just as all do not have constructive positive minds or dimwitted negative ways; all are different.

White females have long been intrigued with Black men, in part as a result of legends portrayed throughout history. In todays' society White women actively seek out Black men whom they are physically, mentally and sexually attracted to. That many White female socialites want to experience relationship with Blacks has been frowned upon for years and in most of their social settings still is. However, now these females are not just looking for sexual encounters with Black men but are also considering them for marriage.

The reason that it appears that more Black men choose to be in relationships with White females than you see White men with Black women is due to the fact that White women have been aggressively pursuing Black men. White men tend to show a slight fear for being in relationships with black woman, which is slowly changing in today's societies. Playboy Magazine's, August, 1969 issue reflects this change as they selected dancer/actress Paula Kelly as their first totally nude female (showing pubic hairs) for the magazine's main feature article.

Many White females have an image of a Black man as big, physically strong and sexually able to satisfy their lust and sometimes their love in a relationship, but other important factor to remember is that Black men are also aggressive mentally and have made many great contributions to this country (discussed in The Education and History Chapter). Black men labored very hard, digging ditches, loading wagons or plowing fields, and other back breaking work, for almost two hundred years which is the main reason they developed physically more than the other races of the generation; they worked at these jobs basically available to them throughout the nineteenth Century.

All marriages, both intra-racial and interracial, cannot be completely free of problems, but in interracial marriages involving persons of two different races, couples have to face certain additional problems besides the routine ones. Most conspicuous amongst these is the stigma of discrimination, which has a greater chance of disrupting the harmony of the conjugal relationships. It is primarily the result of outside influences.

In most interracial marriages, couples are already prepared to put extra effort into the relationship to make it work because of the known odds against the marriage to last. These couples usually try harder as they know they are challenging societal norms. Most interracial marriages last, believe it or not, usually because you have two human beings trying to mentally and emotionally seek the same road as any other couple. When the relationship does not work, it is usually for the same reasons any other marriage does not work. Financial problems etc. may also cause the dissolution!

This chapter is not about persuading anyone that they should marry a person of another race, but it is our earnest hope that it will provide some valuable insight to those who may have been considering entering into interracial marriages. It should be every human's right to choose mates regardless of their race. But one must also be aware of the associated cultural baggage that they have to handle. It is hard enough to find a person who you are compatible with, without circumventing race barriers and self-righteous personal feelings of those who prefer you not to cross such barriers.

There are many interracial married couples that share love and understanding and likewise there are those who share hate and misunderstanding. The later marriages normally don't last longer. Yet if you have more information and experience of life as a couple, be it good or bad, the stronger would be your bonding and more fulfilling would be your relations.

Chapter 6

Food And Beverages

Collard or Mustard Greens, Yams, Red Beans & Rice, Ham Hocks, Pig Feet, Chittlin's and Cornbread are the foods which must readily come to mind when the words "Soul Foods" are mentioned—because they are rib stickin' foods—the type of food which would enable a man to work hard for long hours in the fields. The term "Soul Food" has been around for many generations and probably came into existence through slavery and is a phrase substituted for down home cooking. These were the heavy foods needed to give a family the strength and energy necessary to do the labor demanded of them.

In African culture, when children reached the age of fix in six, the girls and boys were separated and each sent to school like facilities where each was taught their traditional responsibilities. It was the duty of the men to hunt and the women prepared the food. What the women learned depended largely on her tribe's method of getting food. Most of the tribes were farmers or cattle raisers and if the men hunted big game, the woman learned to cook deer, lion, buffalo, elephant, etc. Each tribe specialized in a crop such as yams, rice, okra, corn, cabbage or spinach as a joint venture. The women learned to prepare the tribe's traditional dishes and made them more appealing by serving nuts, beans and vegetables in various ways. Sauces and spices were added to bring out the flavor of dull foods.

Food is one of the few things through which Blacks can identify with their African heritage. After a hard day's work, our appetites need no coaxing; therefore, appetizers are not part of the meal. The slaves brought soul cooking to the southern parts of America from West Africa. Soul food bridges the gap between Blacks all over the world and unites with our African Ancestors. Any meal prepared from the basic food groups of meat, starch and vegetable is classified as "Soul Food", however, what makes it different from cafeteria-style food and meals like steak, baked potato and salad is its quality of being home cooked (a pinch of salt and a dash of pepper) with its natural ingredients (from scratch). In essence, when the statement "I want soul food" is made, it is understood that a good home cooked meal is desired, fresh vegetables and meat—nothing semi-prepared.

Upon arrival in the New World, the slaves found that many of the foods they had eaten in Africa grew in America. The slaves introduced some foods, such as okra, sesame seeds and kidney beans to America. The African cook also brought with her many of the African methods for preparing food.

Pork was considered a delicacy during slavery as wild boars and hogs were plentiful and provided the slaveholder with an inexpensive supply of meat for his family and slaves. After "Hog Killin" time, which usually occurred during the autumn because the cool weather was favorable for storing and preparing the meat, the slaves were rewarded parts of the meat that the slaveholder threw away: feet, ears, intestines (chittlin's), hocks (thighs), tails, maws (stomach) and spareribs. These meats are the backbone of soul food. Like everything else we received secondhand, we were successful in making the best of what was available, just as our ancestors who cooked all parts of the animals they ate.

A look at today's prices for these items will prove how successful we were in making these leftovers tasty and edible. It is a standard joke that when the slaves wanted pork firsthand, they would kill a pig with a blow on the head from a mallet and when questioned about the death of the pig, they would reply that the pig died of Mallitis, and as a result, were given the supposedly diseased pig.

In more recent years, Pork has become denounced meat as we have become more aware of the uncleanliness of this animal and the fact that it is largely responsible for hypertension and other diseases, such as Pellegra, which was common among the slaves who relied on the meals provided by their masters.

Another meat (poultry) most available to us was Chicken—The Preacher's Bird. Chicken can be prepared many ways and is able to adapt to different flavors, making it a very versatile dish. It got its name, "The Preacher's Bird" during slavery—when the Preacher was invited to dinner, it was sure to be Chicken in some form. In West Africa, Chickens were raised for food & trade. The poultry was cooked with collard greens or a stew was made from yam dumplings, which gave it another flavor. Using all parts of the animal, many cooks added the internal organs (liver, gizzards, hearts, head, neck and feet) to make soups and stews. The most frequent way chicken was prepared was by dipping it into a batter and deep fat frying it. No doubt, if the truth were ever known, Colonel Sanders' so called original recipe for fried chicken probably came from his or his ancestor's Black books. Nowadays, many full course appetizing meals can be prepared with chicken. Instead of the traditional "Southern Fried Chicken", such dishes as Baked Chicken, Chicken Legs Parmesan, Ginger Brandy Chicken, and Chicken-in-the-Pot can be served. For the workingwoman who arrives home at 5:00 p.m. and must have dinner on the table by 6:00 p.m. a simple Sherried Chicken Fricassee is a family pleaser.

Africans often roasted meat over an open flame and served it with a sauce and spices, which livened up the taste; this was an early form of what is called "Bar-B-Q" and accounts for our natural ability to "Q meat". Gravies were used to bring out more flavors in food and are prepared by using the juice or drippings of the cooked meat as a base. A sauce is prepared with lemon or vinegar as a base. Most soul meals are served with some type of sauce or gravy, which is important to the meal, as soul food is not a dry food.

Fish, also easily obtained, was usually steamed, deep fat fried, smoked or pickled, and as with other meats and vegetables, the cook used the head, tail and bones to make soups and stews.

Yams play a great part in the Black man's diet. In West Africa, yams were widely cultivated and represented the wealth of a farmer. FU FU (foo foo) was a traditional dish for tribes on the coast of Guinea and was served with a soup or pieces of rams meat or chicken. Yams were boiled, steamed or roasted. Other vegetables (Greens) were steamed, stewed or added to sauces.

Black cooks use onions, tomatoes, carrots, celery, garlic, parsley, seeds and nuts to season foods. A big adjustment made by African American cooks was the type of oil she used. In Africa, the cooks used the oil from various palm trees, which did not grow in the New World. As a substitute, the cooks used the fat from pork.

Being bread eaters, we served some type of bread with every meal. During the sixteenth and eighteenth century, wheat sorghum and corn loco were grinded to make flour and was made into dumplings and biscuits. The term "hoe cake" came about as a result of slaves placing the mixture of uncooked corn meal and water on the blade of a hoe and holding it over an open flame until browned. When this batter is deep fat fried, it is called "hush puppies" and is still often served to compliment fish. This term is believed to have gotten its start during slavery. At picnics, the dogs would hang around the eating tables and whine; these bits of bread were dropped to the dog (to stop his whining) with the remark, "hush puppy". Bread dough is steamed, fried or baked. Today, most bread is prepared with a corn meal base.

In the black community, food is a symbol of love. Whenever friends gather, whatever the occasion, "down home cooking" is in order. Today, as with the case then, food is one of the few joys a Black mother can bestow upon her family. On weekends and holidays, when she has the time and energy needed to prepare delicious soul meals, the family is the recipient of a meal such as the one mentioned at the beginning of this chapter. During the week, when she is too tired from other outside chores, she relies heavily on the African method of frying foods, which takes less time and little preparation.

Blacks and some southern Whites have continued the African tradition of having Black eyed peas (for good luck), Pork, Collard Greens (for money) and Sweet Potato Pie as a New Year's Dinner. A visit to many Black homes and local Black Restaurants will show that many of the basic West Africa cookery methods are still being followed today. The Black cook has added to her cooking abilities great skills in French, Italian, Greek and Mexican cookery as a result of cooking for other ethnic groups.

Most of our beverages were homemade. A type of beer was made from rice and grains of corn and was served warm. Many different kinds and qualities of wine were made from corn, sugar cane and palm trees. The palm wines, which came from the same tree as the palm cooking oil, was served at many important social and religious ceremonies. Alcohol, usually strong in taste, was brewed from corn and wheat and was often used as remedies for colds, fevers, etc. Many illnesses have been cured with remedies using homemade liquor as a base. Having little exposure to various types of teas and imported wines, these beverages were not common among Blacks; however, more recently these items are being added to the menus and dinner tables of many Black homes and restaurants. During the era when Root Beer, Coke and Strawberry were few of the common flavors available in soft drinks, many of us preferred the not so strong, smooth taste of "Red (Strawberry) Soda Water".

With such good foods and beverages still being served regularly and in the absence of "physical field labor", it's no wonder our physiques are generally sturdy and healthy looking.

Chapter 7

Religious Views

Religion has played a major role in the evolution of cultures from the 1ˢᵗ recorded history and has significantly affected the lives of Blacks not only in America but even before they were brought to America from Africa. The Black churches are the oldest and largest Black organizations around the world, and leaders in the Black communities have come from all segments of black society, from millionaires to slaves, and everything in between. No matter how you look at it, Blacks have been a major part of American history and so is the Black church, at one time; its members were more than 20% of the total population of the nation. Most American Blacks have ancestors dating further back in American history than those of the Irish, Italians, Pollack's, Germans, Scandinavians and Spanish.

The African Methodist Baptist Church first came into existence (not officially) around 1733, although they were only allowed to worship fragments of their African homeland's traditional religious teachings and beliefs such as tribal voodooist, witch doctor's chants, sun worshipping rituals, and other African tribal worshiping doctrines. They smuggled in Bibles and had to hide them in fear of their slave owners becoming aware that they were secretly reading the Bible. If they were found to be reading the Bible they would be punished or killed, for it was believed by slave owners that Blacks did not have souls and considered them heathens without the rights to be taught the word of the church though Bible. Most feared that if Blacks were taught to be Christians from the Bible, they would consider themselves free people and equal to Whites.

It was not until the "Great Awakening" and the massive series of outdoor revivals and camp meetings that swept the country in 1733 that the Christian religion became a critical factor for the Blacks in America. From 1786 to 1788 in Philadelphia, Richard Allen and a handful of Black Christians, who were unwilling to separate their roots and religion from their dignity, formed the first organized denomination of the African Methodist Episcopal Church. Since the Black church was the only means available to organize Black council, it soon became a stepping-stone and training ground for Black political leaders and social organizers.

Christianity is a "White people's religion" and is the White people's planted seed to manipulate and serve the White people's personal end game. Therefore, it could not be used as the base foundation to control people in Africa, as the Islamic advance was three-pronged; proselytizing missions claiming one brotherhood; widespread intermarriages and creating concubines with African women, based on the Muslim system of polygamy; and forceful conversions at the point of a sword.

Christianity used the Crusades to invade, conquer and steal relics, which they hid in the catacombs of Rome where many can be found today. They destroyed all religious doctrines, symbols of the areas faith in Asia and Africa, using missionaries to brain wash the natives of the region into believing that Christianity was the only true faith, and the images they used of Jesus Christ and God were of a White man, that is still used today.

White people over time changed the color of Christ in images he is portrayed as, from a dark skinned person to a White person. How could a man that was born and raised just above the Northern tip of Africa and Southern Asia where he spent most of his adult life be White skinned? The people of Northern Africa or Southern Asia are of dark complexion simply due to the climate and the norm for people living in those areas.

This is not to say Jesus was black, but I am making the point he had to be of darker skin color, if not, for no other reason than he lived for many years basically in desert country that is not known for White inhabitants. White people, for the purpose of confirming that Jesus was not a person of color, intentionally implemented this deceit.

The doctrine based on the cross of Jesus Christ, followed the Muslim Crescent doctrine and the cloak of Christianity was a convenient hiding place for those who had other designs on controlling converting the religious views of others. Hence, the drive to convert African people to Christianity, conversion meant far more than conversion to Christianity; as in the case of Islam, it meant changing ideal into the reality of White people's image, their ideals and value system. The real object of worship for those who converted turned out to be neither Jesus Christ nor God, but the controlling tool of Western men and Western civilization over others.

Most people never stop to look and wonder why it is that most Blacks have never built an unforgiving deep hatred for their forefathers' enslavers, nor do they wonder why blacks on a larger scale (due to many prejudiced whites) have not started a major race war. It is not because they do not have the means, but because teaching of right and wrong that their faith asks them to forgive for the better good of the race. Black people are religious by nature as it is part of their linage to strive for the good in all men and is part of their upbringing since the beginning of history.

The hatred that some Black people have for White people was developed by past actions of White people and their ancestors. Hate is like one bad apple in a barrel, it can affect all the other apples in that barrel. Many Black people appear angry and sometimes can be prone to start riots, fighting, or just raising ruckus, but this is not just because their forefathers were enslaved, but how many White people still tend to treat (Blacks) today as if they were still slaves.

Blacks feel that White peoples attitude towards them is "that they believe are better than Black people". Black people have worked hard at demonstrating they are as talented, artistic, athletic, and inelegant as any other race with the help of the church, schools, and their faith in God. The Black church has held Black people together and has been the life guide for many Black leaders, men such as Bishop Henry McTeil Turner (before and after Civil War) Adam Clayton Powell, Martin Luther King, Ralph Abernathy, Jesse Jackson and the list does not end!

The most popular religions among Black people are Methodist, Baptist, Protestant, and Church of God in Christ, Catholic and Islam in America. Many Whites have become more familiar with the Islamic religion, greatly due to exposure of high profile Black members achievements like,

Muhammad Ali (Cassius Clay), Kareem Abdul Jabbar (Lew Alcindor) Malcolm X, and others who have chosen Islam as the religion of their faith. Muhammad Ali converted to Sunni Islam in 1975. Black Muslims, who are the American hybrid of the Muslim faith, have increased the numerical strength and power of the Muslim nation that is recognized by White people as a force to be reckoned with in America, during these trying times. The Blacks are slowly adopting views and ideals of traditional Muslims while still maintaining their adherence to the structure of the National Objectives.

The leaders of the Nation of Islam teach followers to "do for self" socially, spiritually and economically. Wallace D. Fard Muhammad founded the Nation, coincidently on July 4, 1930 and in less than 60 years of organized efforts; the nation has built a solid financial base and continues to prosper today, despite the recent death of their leader and the founder's right hand, born Elijah Robert Poole, known as The Honorable Elijah Muhammad.

More than half of the Black population belongs to the Baptist religion, the rest are split between Methodist, Protestant, Catholic, Muslim, etc. Others may not officially participate in any organized faith, but one or the other faith dose influence decisions they make in their life and in times of need; also, the faith reminds them that they are no different than any other person or race.

There seems to be confusion about the origin of "Black Jewish people" in World history, however, the fact is that they are from the same historic origin as Black and White Arabs— who lived in exactly the same areas as history dictates and where the birth of the religions took place. For we have known that Jewish people live in Africa from the earliest times and that Africans lived in Palestine from the earliest times.

History tells us that Jewish people never engaged themselves in the general enslavement of Black people that occurred in the western world. In warfare, either side might have captured segments of the population to be marched off to work for the victorious nation, a notable instance being the Jewish capacity in Egypt and their later emancipation and return under the leadership of Moses. Not only did many Black and Colored Jews crossed the Red Sea with Moses, but also doubtlessly many Blacks, such as the wife of the official Lawgiver, converted to Jewish faith.

Furthermore, as in the case of Arabs, we often confuse race with religion, the people we call "Jews" indiscriminately are Hebrews by race and Jewish by religion. Anyone can be Jewish, but not a Hebrew. The Hebrews and the Arabs are both decedents of White Semitic peoples, and none of the offspring of non-Hebrews and non-Arabs, or adherents to either religion, will ever change this absolute fact. After all those centuries of racial mixing, there was nothing unusual about the appearance of great Black Colored leaders in Palestine or anywhere else in Asia, including from time to time their rise in kingship of Israel, Syria (Aram), Mesopotamia, etc.

But today White Jews (Hebrews) and White Arabs remain exactly what they always were—White; and this is why the one who dose not to know this truth fails to comprehend why there is a racial crisis today in Israel between the ruling White Jews and the Colored (Black) Jews who have migrated to Israel from the afore-mentioned African and Asian lands. There are many Colored adherents of Judaism from Arab countries; many who chose not to become Muslims. It is quite useless and unnecessary to try to persuade people that either Jesus Christ or the Prophet Muhammad were "Black" or even "Colored" as there is no known portrait of either to verify that to be the truth, but common sense has to dictate that both had to be persons of color, not White.

African religions as well as Black churches have always projected a great deal of emotional feelings of their members, both mentally and physically and many of our leading Evangelists both White and Black who started as preachers in the Evangelist church, preach fire and brimstone sermons. These sermons are the foundation of the Black churches. They work themselves up both mentally and physically to a point of generating spiritual feelings in themselves and those around them during these sermons.

When their emotions overwhelm them, as many in the Black church would say, God chooses to speak to them at that particular time and asks them to stand up and scream, shout with joy and happiness. That's where the term "shouting" came into being as a word relating to the emotions of the Black church.

The church, its teachings and faith in God are rooted deep in Black history and at one point in time it was all they had to hope and strive for a better existence. Faith in God was their only asset as their enslavers not only forcefully deprived them of their homes but also trapped and caged them; and after enslaving they were left with little or no hope of salvation.

Black people that have attended White churches, see them as houses with out spirit, warmth, enthusiasm, and emotions and very little joy. When men have to fight for freedom physically and mentally from another man, emotional, joyful faith is what gives the oppressed the requisite hope and that hope comes from worshipping God. After all, it was God who gave life and freedom to all men and it has never been the rightful choice of any man to snatch that freedom for their own personal gain.

Views on religion and Black church are just footnotes as many Blacks worship in White and Black churches today. The worshipping by blacks in white denominations first came about following the Civil War. The white church was the only tool besides the Bible that blacks had to learn what they could about Christianity. In just about all religions, blacks are and have been involved as leaders in taking the messages of God and passing them on.

There have been many religious Black church cult leaders that have influenced Black and White followers like Father Divine, who was the founder of the Peace Mission cult, a religious movement whose followers believed in his divinity. The cult, according to the late Father Divine, was a cooperative agency whose main purpose was providing faith and services for those in need, such as the low cost housing for believers during the Depression of 1930.

Some Blacks achieved high positions in predominantly White denominations. In 1966, Rev. Harold R. Perry was consecrated Bishop of the Roman Catholic Church in New Orleans. Rev. John M. Burgess was appointed the first black bishop of the Protestant Episcopal Church. Dr. Thomas Kilgore was elected president of the American Baptist convention in 1969, becoming the first Black person to head the 1.5 million member denomination. To add to the growing unity in mankind, the predominantly white Catholic denominations have taken steps to incorporate Black rituals such as celebrations of African mass in Roman Catholic services.

There are many views on religion involving Black people discussed in this chapter. They are only meant to provide a small insight for the people who want to understand more about the religious views of black people in America during the sixties and seventies. For further evaluation of religion in Black communities you may use the information given in this chapter and in the book sources listed in the Introduction. This will hopefully provide a better understanding of what the Bible says "Love thy neighbor as you would love yourself, the Son and the Holy Ghost, thy God" and what it truly means to those that chose to enslave others.

Chapter 8

Ethnic Fashions

How does one explain "Ethnic Fashions", what they are today and how they were brought to popularity by Black people, in movies, musical entertainment and other famed fields. Of all the chapters I've written, I found this one the most interesting and hard to put in words.

To dress is to cover or adorn the body. The style of dress tells a lot about an individual such as his role in society, self-identity and the socialization process, etc. During the early settlement days of the New World, Whites brought with them not only their puritanical manners, but also the dress similarities of the Englishman. Their color patterns were very subdued (Black, Browns Navy, and Gray). As a rule, businessmen, secretaries, schoolteachers, librarians, etc. adhered to these color patterns. Those were the people who influenced the dress code for "respectable" people. It was established that any woman who wore colors such as red was a worldly woman and it was completely unheard of for a man to wear colors such as pink, light blue, green, etc.

"Respectable" women and girls wore skirts below the knee (ankle length) with long sleeve white blouses and jackets. Everyone looked alike in his or her form of dress. Anyone who went against the norm in his dress was often avoided and regarded as being anti-establishment. Only entertainers were permitted the scarlet colors, as their dress was regarded as a part of their working wardrobe. Even many movie actors and actresses adhered to the subdued colors as much as possible.

After World War II, people began to appear a bit more relaxed in their dress and creativeness in clothing became acceptable. Paris soon became the center of attention of the fashion world, with Western designers duplicating the latest styles.

Blacks have held their own style in the fashion world from the time they wore the hand-me-downs of Western White Americans to this "Superfly Epoch of the 70's". Blacks have always dressed in colors, being inherently accustomed to bright bold prints and solid colors. During the hand-me-downs period, I can imagine Blacks receiving and having to wear brown pants with a red shirt, and their ancestral instinct from their African heritage caused them to match with red socks. Remembering what they could from their African Culture, Blacks were able to remake these hand-me-downs into styles of their own. Being creative, alterations to these hand-me-downs were made into such styles as the Zoot Suit; Peg Pants; Chemise and Sack Dresses, Tent Dresses and many more which were made popular by such personalities as Louis Jordan, Cab Calloway, Bessie Smith, Billie Holiday, etc. long before Whites were able to make the real money through mass production of these marketable items.

This stereotype "naked savage" image was applied to Africans because they had no hang ups about their bodies. Being free of hang-ups, there was no need for members of certain tribes to wear clothing. However, variations to dress are due largely to climate location and other environmental influences.

Because they were uninhibited, African descendants regard dressing as an act of adoring the body and take more than average pride in their style of dress. Having a natural instinct for bold, bright colors, Blacks were considered outlandish dressers who just didn't know any better. In fact, it is self-pride that makes Blacks seek out styles that are full of zest and add a little glide to the stride and puts pep in the step.

The next time you are dressed and feel confident in your outward appearance, take note of the pride in your walk, notice the confident way you talk and also notice how consciously you feel good about yourself. (Go ahead, let loose, we all have outfits that make us feel like we are on top of the world and really look our best.)

Afro Americans have refined the cuts of suits, the taper, etc. and have added more colors to their wardrobe. The interesting fact is that the puritanical mode of dressing has become more relaxed as a result of close contact with other ethnic groups, the exchange of ideas and other influences which effect ones environment. Westerners have begun to accept pinks, greens, reds and other such colors for men and the fact that women in professional fields no longer have to be subjected to matronly looks be the subdued colors she was once forced to wear.

With the coming of Black awareness in the 50's and 60's, African Americans began to take on the look of their ancestors. They discarded hairstyles such as Conks, Page Boys and ended the usage of rats and pomades and took on wearing the Afro and Natural hairstyles, which a proud image dictates as being natural. This was the start of revolutionary creations like the Dashikis and African look alike accessories (here again, white westerners manufactured and profited from our awareness as they mass produced these styles). These styles brought unity, pride, and respect to Blacks all over the country, as it enabled us to relate in a heritage way to our ancestors. While an African code of dress has not been adopted in its entirety by Afro Americans, it has given Blacks a sense of direction which enables them to remove the stigmatism that prevailed in their minds for many years as they were brainwashed into thinking they had no culture other than what was being exposed to them through media and slave owners.

Becoming aware of their background has given them the opportunity to decide for themselves how they want to project their inner selves, which is what dress is all about. Certain African tribes used coronets and boas on gala occasions long before they became stylish accessories of the Western Fashion World. The wrapping of the head with printed and solid scarves is traditional apparel for African descendants and is very fashionable today for both men and women.

Black pimps are largely responsible for the "Superfly Epoch" of the 70's. They made popular the use of otherwise forbidden colors in men's suits, the platform high-heeled shoes and the leather carrying bags for men. Pimps originally wore this style of dressing, however, as attitudes towards dress became more relaxed, these uniformed "tools of trade" became fads for many.

The primary difference between the styles of Blacks wears and whites wear is that Blacks are very flashy in their dress whereas Whites tend to be more conservative, projecting a low profile. For example, take two identical suits; give one to a Black individual and the other to a White individual. Chances are that due to cultural traditions, the Black individual will add an accessory which will call attention to the outfit, giving it flair and uniqueness, such as a wild scarf, pin, shirt, etc., whereas a White individual will be more apt to keep strictly to the basic necessities required by the outfit, a solid shirt, little or no jewelry, etc.

Many of us did not know that the French Foreign Legion is in Africa, which gives you some idea of the control that France had in Africa. This explains why Paris is the fashion capital of the world. The designers in Paris modified the style of African dress for both males and females to conform to the style of the puritanical western patterns. For example, take the hooded Kaftans, and Bermuda shorts, as they are known today, were originated in Africa where they were used by some Africans to keep the body cool and the sun and wind out of the face.

The 1960's and 70's have given the world such Black Fashion designers as Stephen Burrows, Willi Smith, Scott Barrie, Jon Weston, Milton Farquhar, whose specialty is handbags and luggage, and Donald Hubbard, who has been designing shoes for men for more than 18 years. All these designers use flair of African design in their styles and stick more to the bright bold prints and solids and accessorize their creations with matching scarves, for wrapping the head, and African look jewelry.

Chapter 9

Black Talent

The United States is the only country in the world wherein the majority of the people really have opportunity to showcase talents they have developed. This does not mean they will always have the chance to earn a living performing their talents, nor does it mean that they will get credit for their talent, as many may deserve. Black people, through their talents in sports, music, entertainment, creativeness, inventions, etc., have given America many achievements that are used in the day-to-day lives of its citizens.

I would bet if I were a betting person that most Americans are unaware that many of the enjoyments they relish are because of the Black people who have a major part in their existence. Deserts and snacks such as ice cream and potato chips are just two of them. Hyram S. Thomas, a chef in Saratoga, New York, created potato chips, and a confectioner, Augustus Jackson, first made one of America's favorite deserts, good old ice cream from Philadelphia, PA.

Pele, the number one soccer in the world is a Black person and is also the highest paid athlete in the world at the time of writing this book. The reason he is the highest paid athlete is that he has perfected his skills at the game of soccer so well that people all around the world stand in long lines to see him play, and he is highly sought after for advertising campaign endorsements around the world as a result. The most popular person in the world is also another Black athlete, entertainer, teacher and philosopher and one of the most powerful men alive, Muhammad Ali.

If you will just look around you, despite the odds against doing so, you will see that Blacks have mastered arts originally created by White people and added new twist and refinements of their own for additional perfection of that art. Of all the people that inhabited the 13 rebellious American colonies in 1776, Black people were viewed as the least likely to make any substantial cultural contribution. With all odds and the majority of White people against them, Black people have continued to contribute to American culture. As far back in history as 1746, a slave named Lucy Terry wrote a poem commemorating an Indian raid on the Massachusetts town of Deerfield exhibited in the Library of Congress. Black people have had to learn to do things better than White people in order to be classified "just as good". This meant that no matter what their chosen field was, they had to master it as well as be extraordinary in order to receive recognition.

On the subject of music, let's not forget the only original music that America can rightfully claim as originating in this country is Ragtime, which gave us Blues, R & B and Jazz. Everyone in America should be aware that Blacks are responsible for these achievement, and it was not until 1972 when a Black entertainer received an Oscar for the best musical score; ("The String", the song was called "The Entertainer"), influenced by Scott Joplin was honored as the major ragtime innovator and composer.

For centuries, Blacks have mastered every sport presented to them. Everyone knows that gladiators were faced with the best competition a country had to offer, and he was usually black. He was not necessarily always the biggest, but he was able to master his weapons and prepare himself physically and mentally whereas his major objective and goal was self-preservation and a strong will to survive. This usually kept him a champion for many years, until he gained his freedom. The greatest known gladiator was not a slave but a warrior, Hannibal, who was also Black.

Now, nearly 200 years later, record books will show that black people hold 75% of records in most sports, something readers can view for themselves. All basketball fans know Wilt "The Stilt" Chamberlin, the player that holds most professional basketball records including the only player to score 100 points in a game and averaged fifty points and fifty rebounds in a season and Bill Russell who is a living legion has more championship rings than any player in NBA history to date. Football fans will always remember Jim Brown, Gale Sayers, Night "Train" Lane, Deacon Jones who are only a few of many great NFL Hall of Fame players, that have made football the game it is today. Blacks had to reach higher goals and perform better than White athletes in order to be recognized for achievements in sports, entertainment, are any other activities.

To date people of color are still not given the same chances to get leading roles on TV, stage or movies and the Oscars, Emmys, Grammys have not been equally awarded to people of color, for years. Think about it this way; If you start first, you generally will be the first one to be recognized, but if you start last and finish first shouldn't that rate more recognition? But does not always happen for Black people that finish first? Black people have always found joy in entertaining others, just as their ancestors have done for hundreds of years. The love and feelings of happiness in making others happy and overjoyed, is and has always been a gift of joy for Black people.

Blacks have long been noted for being relaxed and carefree, just as Whites are stereotyped as being tense with little emotions. The main reason for this could be because the majority of Whites don't really get into entertaining themselves to the point of inner-relaxation. Black people have contributed greatly to the progress of America in the past and present, fall for the good and betterment of America.

Below are the lyrics of a song written in 1972, by Sirron Kyles one of the authors of this book, "I wanted to share the lyrics with those that read this book and as how I feel about working towards unity as we move forward together in America.

"BEAUTIFUL BEIGE"
(Original Lyrics)

Happiness, Peace, and Universal Love
Are things you can fine right here on earth and
In Heaven above
Sooner or later we shall see a change over each of us,
Including me
There will be no Black, White, Brown Yellow or Red
The Only color of man, will be beautiful beige, beautiful beige

Love, Peace, and happiness are the only ways
I can only hope that all people of the earth,
Will be as one to see that day

There is a real chance that by then,
Instead of fighting each other we can and will all be friends.
And as we live as one the world will grow older in time
And as that happens all the people on earth will age
When that day comes there will be no Black, White
Brown Yellow or Red, as all on earth will be a beautiful beige
Then there will be no reasons for people to be
Known as Black, White, Brown, yellow or Red as All chances of
discrimination when that
Happens, will be dead.
That is what real unity is and the only way that when these days
Occur, it will change discrimination will never exist in man's
head
If you and me could all see the true happiness and change that
lies in
Our future days
Then you would know that the color of us all would
End up and I mean all beauty races full Beige
If the color of every man skin is no longer seen as Black, White,
Brown, yellow or
Red, but a blend of all races skins colors then and only then we
will all be as one, the color,
Beautiful Beige.

Sirron

It does take talent to realize that we as a people of the world are not in total unity, but it takes even more talent to realize that just by man's ability to stay alive and working to bring unity to the world, that through time, the colors of the world as found in mankind today will blend into the color beige; physically, spiritually and mentally, colors of unity.

With the knowledge of total unity, which should be on all of our minds, and imagine if we as people reach our true identities and reach height of advancements for all to be one God just by blending hearts with love not hate. If we as a people could eliminate hatred and realize is the way to offset the strong forces of evil that influences man to create Hate.

Black talents are not the only talents the world has to offer that will lead to the happiness and unity of mankind, but realizing the knowledge that all races have a part in the puzzle of life that we all must strive to put it all together, in order for the Love of man to work as one.

Conclusion

Some might say writing this book will create animosity and hate; others will criticize the book because they dislike Black people because of the guilt they feel about how their ancestors treated Black people's ancestors. Others will praise the book because of the information it shares, but whatever critics may say, the reason for us writing this book was the hopes of providing people that read it, a better insight and understanding of Black people that lived in the sixties and seventies. We are inviting everyone who may have a curiosity and interest in reading about Black people during this era, read the book and after reading it we hope you have a new way of interacting with anyone of color who might move next door to you, or for that matter, friends of color that your son or daughter might bring home to dinner.

We are sure most people want to be prepared to live along side and understand all people especially Black people of America and around the world to live in unity. For the authors writing this book was all about Love and Unity, Not Hate.

Look at this bit of logic even though you might think it is strange. Man gives better unity to everything on earth; even dogs, there may be twenty different kinds, but basically he still classifies them as dogs. You still have those whites that still and will separate and segregate humans from their own kind, with some to go as far as saying and believing that blacks are not human and are ignorant animals. Yet, these people go to church and supposedly classify themselves as Christians who follow the God of Love, Really.

Would this not make this type of person a hypocrite and most certainly not a believer of God's words?

The black men and women, single or married, are very proud people, this has to be the first thing they gained in themselves as people because without self-pride, how can you will yourself to advance in any manner?

To the people who use discrimination as a tool in life and will not change their ways, it might be better for them to become color blind until that day when they see all people the same, just saying.

"What If All People That Hate People Of Color, People of Different Genders, And The Poor, All Had Heart Attacks, And The Only People Around That Could Provide CPR To Save Them Are The People They Hate; Would The People That Had The Heart Attack Still Hate The People That Saved Them?"

Sirron

Photo Gallery

A Revealing Visual Photo Interstation Insight Into The Life Of Black Americans During the Sixties And Seventies And Before

Photo Page 1
Achievements

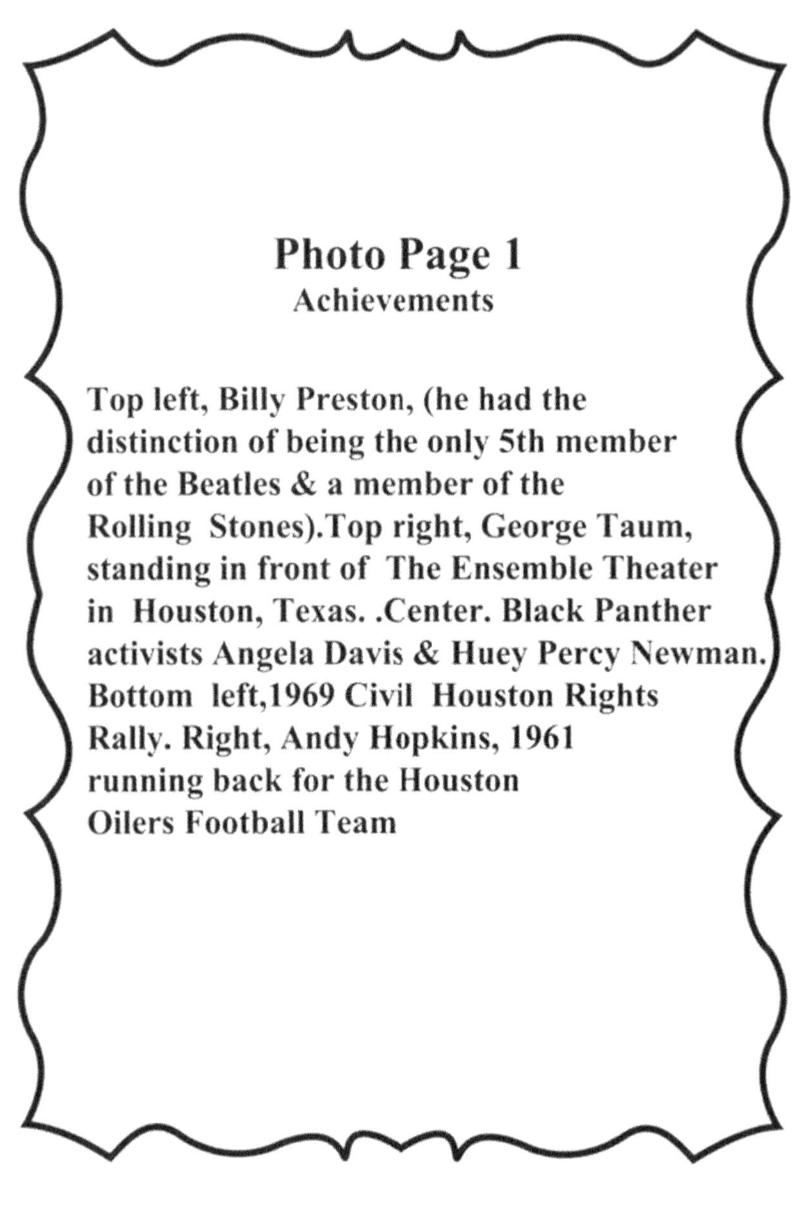

Top left, Billy Preston, (he had the
distinction of being the only 5th member
of the Beatles & a member of the
Rolling Stones).Top right, George Taum,
standing in front of The Ensemble Theater
in Houston, Texas. .Center. Black Panther
activists Angela Davis & Huey Percy Newman.
Bottom left,1969 Civil Houston Rights
Rally. Right, Andy Hopkins, 1961
running back for the Houston
Oilers Football Team

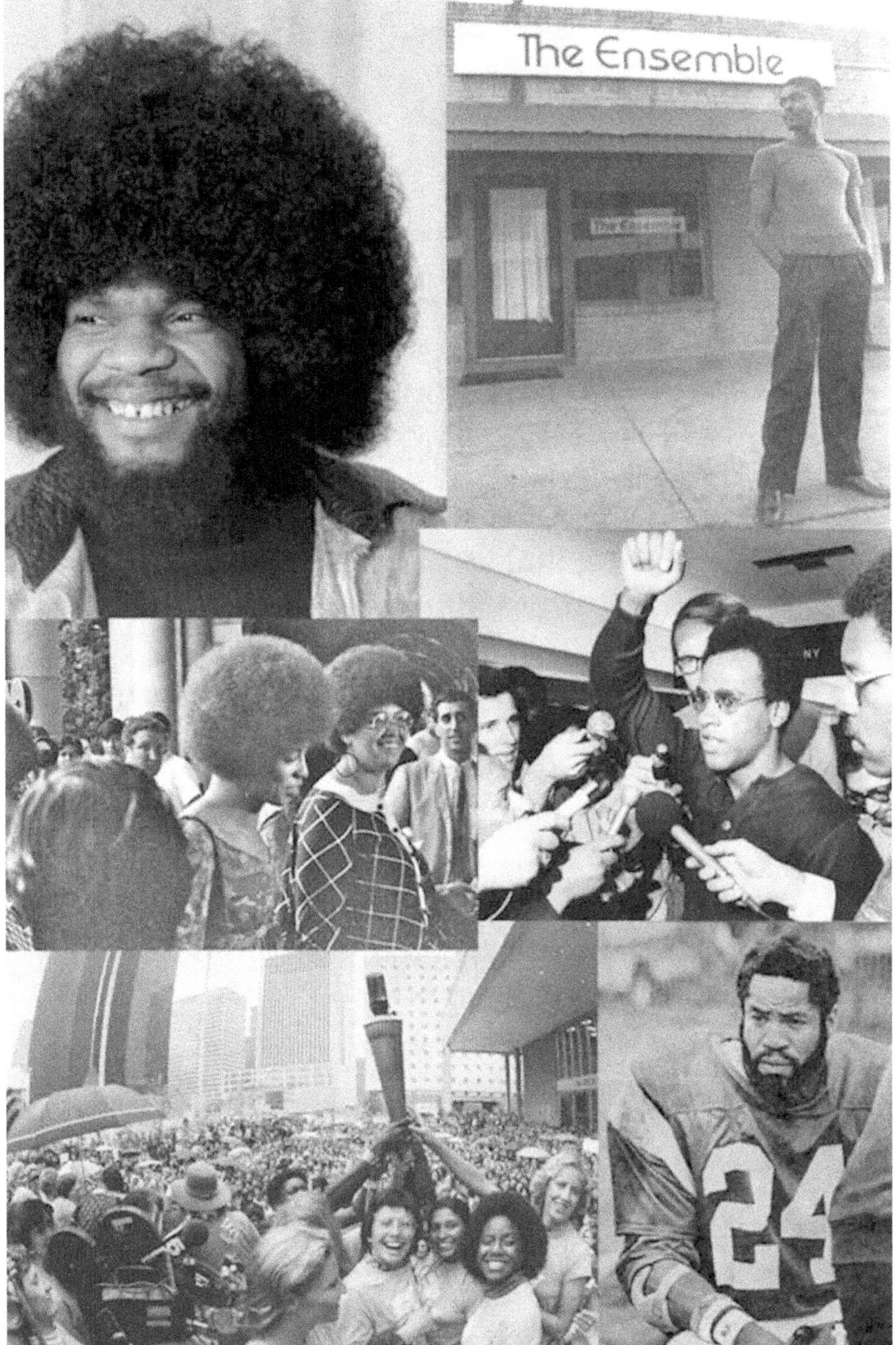
The Ensemble

Photo Page 2
Refused Induction History

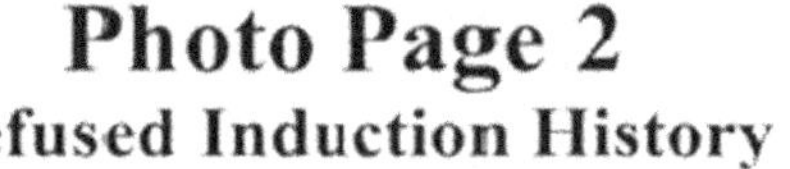

Top, April 28, 1967, Muhammad Ali, (Cassius Marcellus Clay Jr.) Ali, changed his name in 1964 after joining the Nation of Islam) went before the military induction officials inside Houston, Texas's Military entrance processing station building, Ali shown here at the top and refused to step forward for induction when his name was called, due to his religious convictions. Below, Sirron Kyles, (left) one of the books authors with James "Skully" Austin, 1972 (right) was the next person in line behind Ali at the induction. James went on to serve in the US Army, as a promoter for Soul Train and a part of Ali's entourage

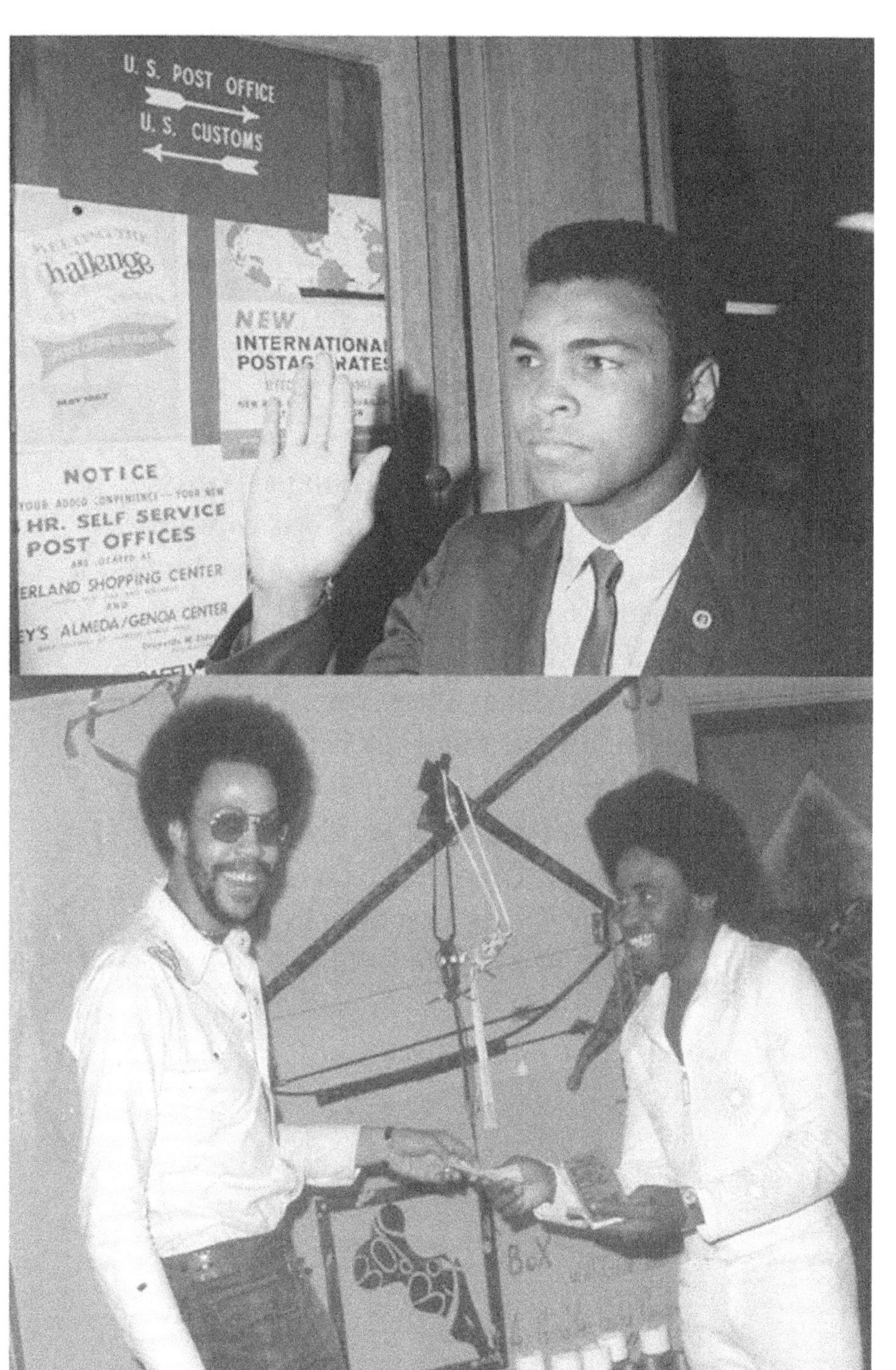
U. S. POST OFFICE
U. S. CUSTOMS
hallenge
NEW
INTERNATIONAL
POSTAG RATES
NOTICE
HR. SELF SERVICE
POST OFFICES
ERLAND SHOPPING CENTER
EY'S ALMEDA/GENOA CENTER

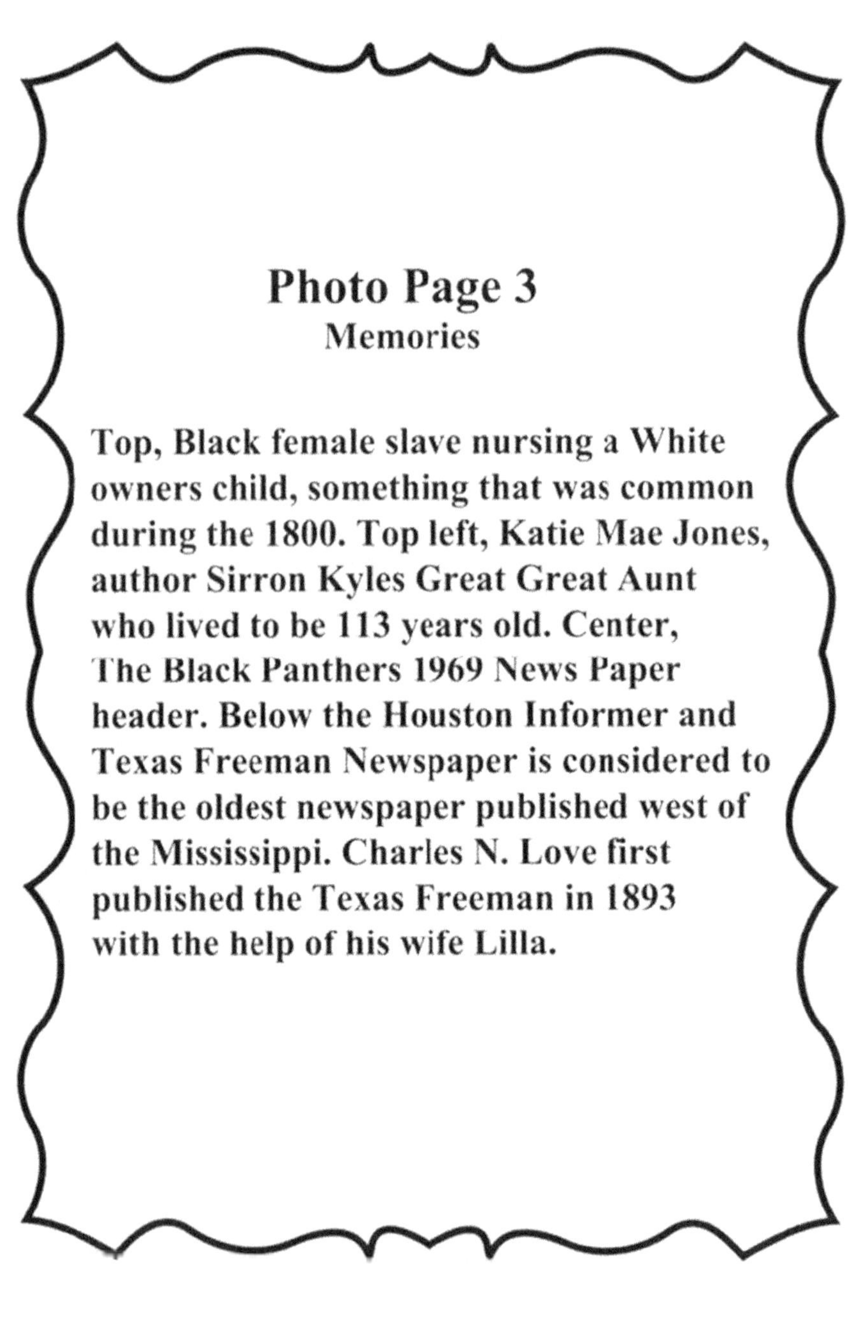

Photo Page 3
Memories

Top, Black female slave nursing a White owners child, something that was common during the 1800. Top left, Katie Mae Jones, author Sirron Kyles Great Great Aunt who lived to be 113 years old. Center, The Black Panthers 1969 News Paper header. Below the Houston Informer and Texas Freeman Newspaper is considered to be the oldest newspaper published west of the Mississippi. Charles N. Love first published the Texas Freeman in 1893 with the help of his wife Lilla.

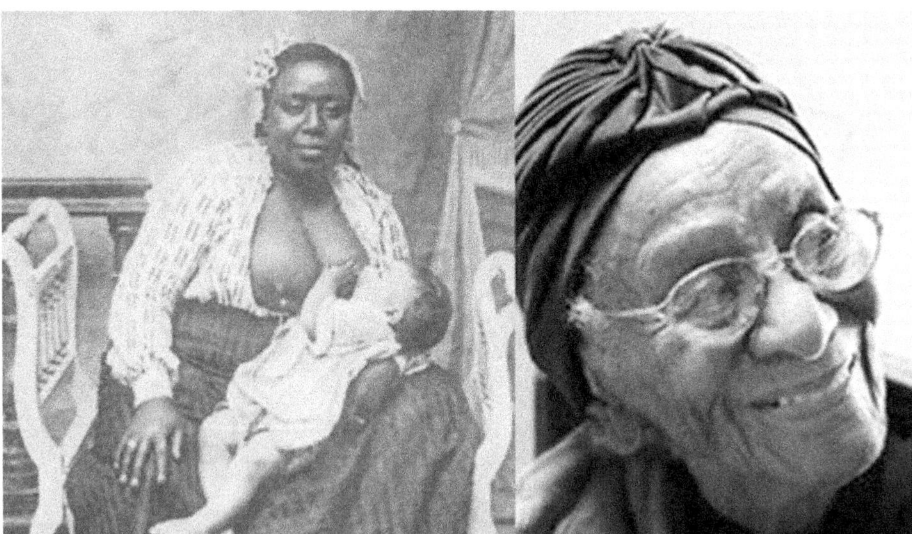

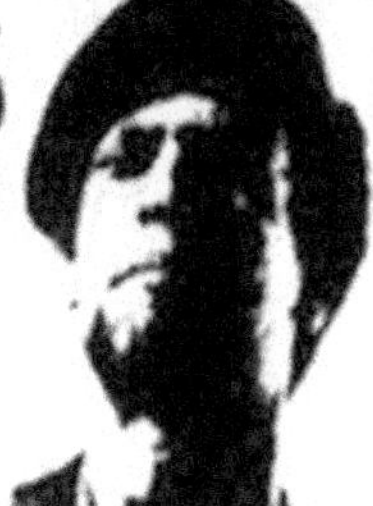

THE HOUSTON INFORMER
5 Cts.
AND
THE TEXAS FREEMAN
A WEEKLY NEWSPAPER FOR ALL THE PEOPLE
OUR PHONE NUMBER IS PRESTON
7916

VOL. XIII — HOUSTON, TEXAS, SATURDAY, DECEMBER 12, 1931 — NUMBER 29

INFORMER'S 2ND PRIMARY BRIEF FILED

A Non-Partisan Political Meeting Held In Nation's Capital By Negro Group

DEMO CHAIRMAN

HOUSTON MOURNS SUDDEN DEATH OF YATES TEACHER

SUCCEEDING

Document Is Accepted By The Supreme Court Over Protest Of White Demos

MARYLAND MOB BURNS INJURED AND DYING MAN

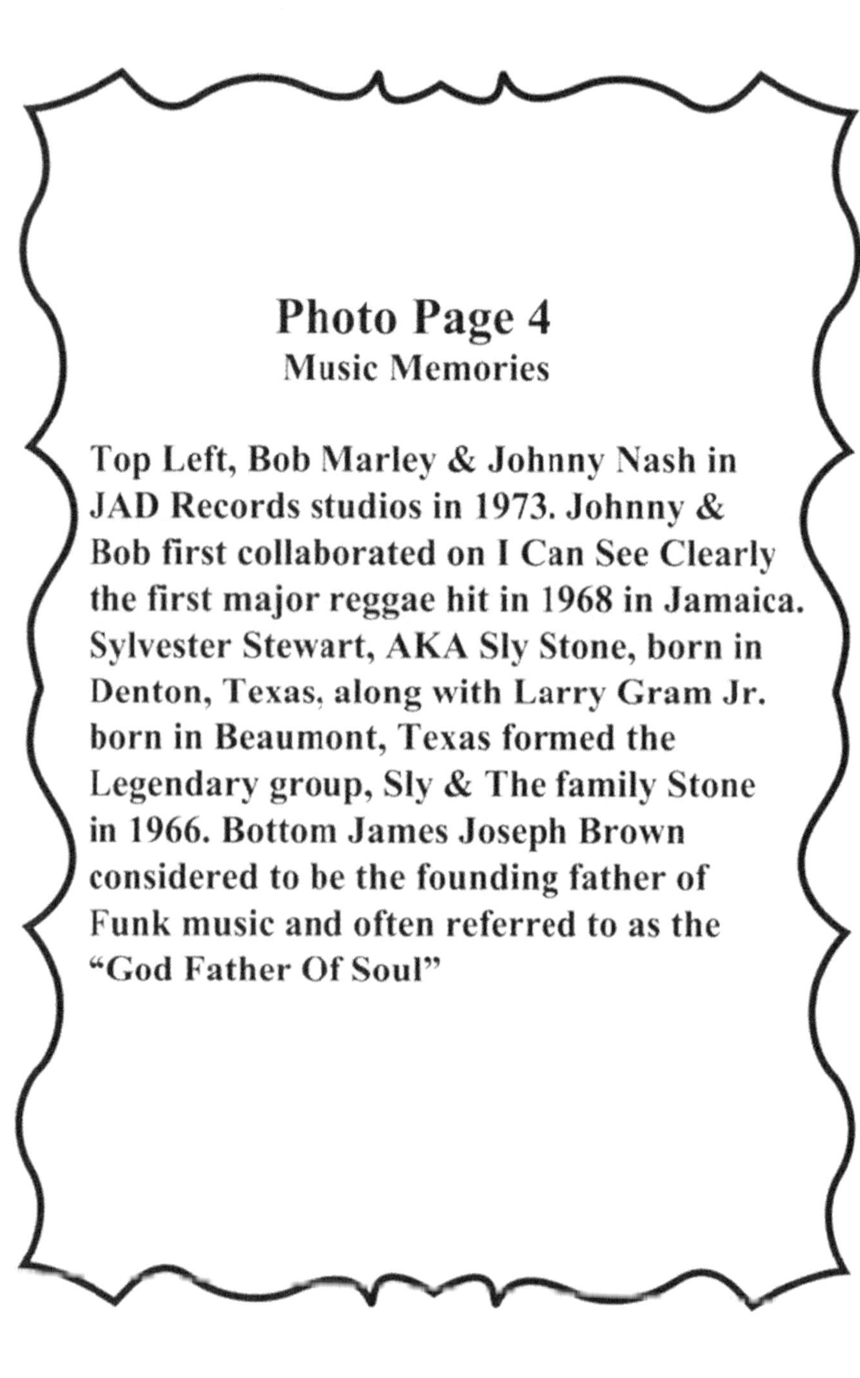

Photo Page 4
Music Memories

Top Left, Bob Marley & Johnny Nash in JAD Records studios in 1973. Johnny & Bob first collaborated on I Can See Clearly the first major reggae hit in 1968 in Jamaica. Sylvester Stewart, AKA Sly Stone, born in Denton, Texas, along with Larry Gram Jr. born in Beaumont, Texas formed the Legendary group, Sly & The family Stone in 1966. Bottom James Joseph Brown considered to be the founding father of Funk music and often referred to as the "God Father Of Soul"

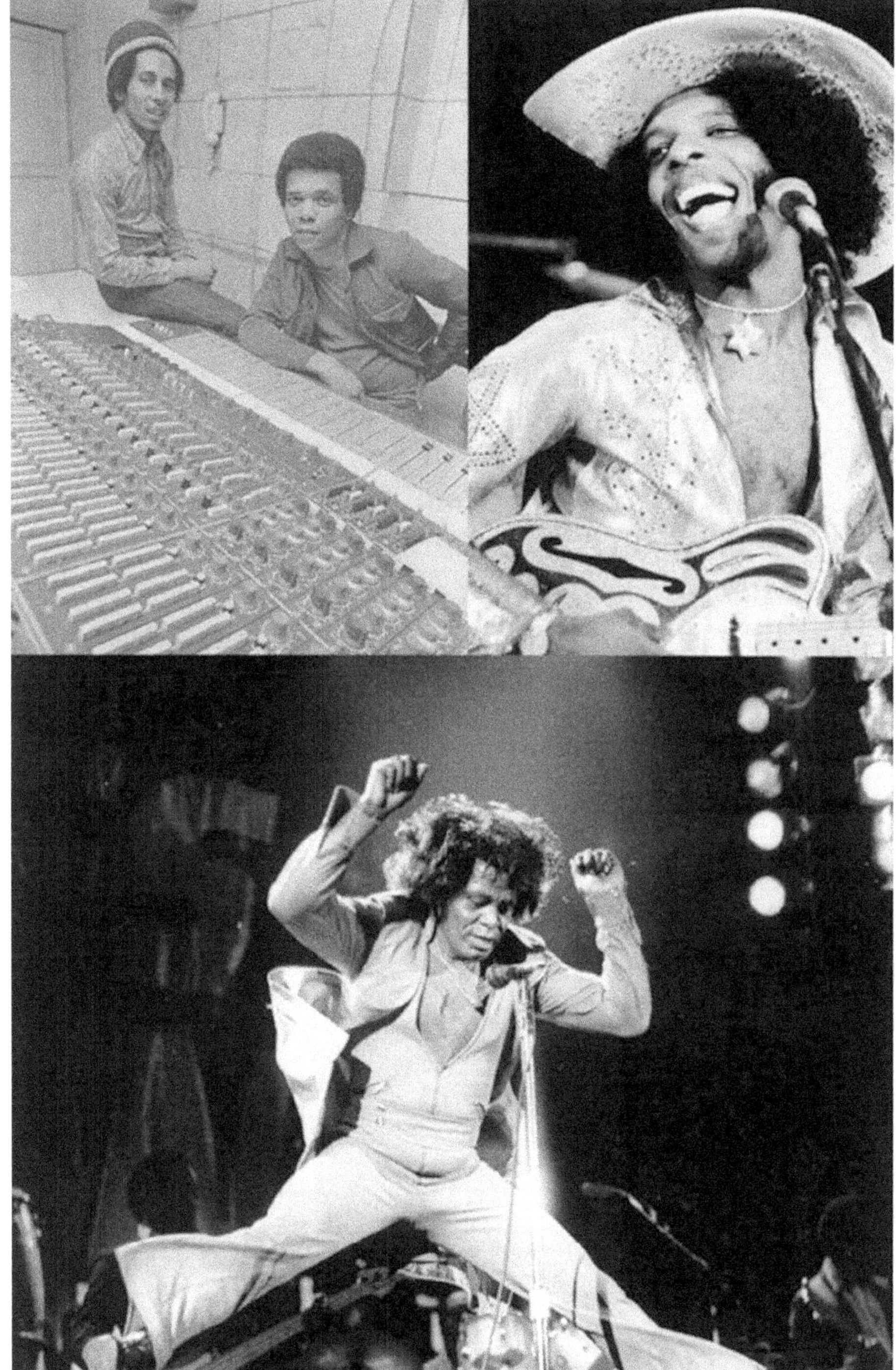

Photo Page 5
Cooking

African Americans have cooked for and
taught, White Americans families as
slaves for centuries. Many of the recipes
found in American Cook Books, originated
from African American Slave's recipes.
Many food products use African American
images and names to market their products;
Uncle Ben's rice, Aunt Jamima pancakes etc.
Below center Mary Mcleod Bethune
Institute1860 help formally trained
students in the fine art of cooking. Top left
head Chef Joe Erwin Kyles, 1955,
3rd from left at Yea Old College Inn,
a prestigious restaurant near Rice University
in Houston, Texas 1950. Many
of the recipes he created were use in a
cook booked released in 1956 by the owner.

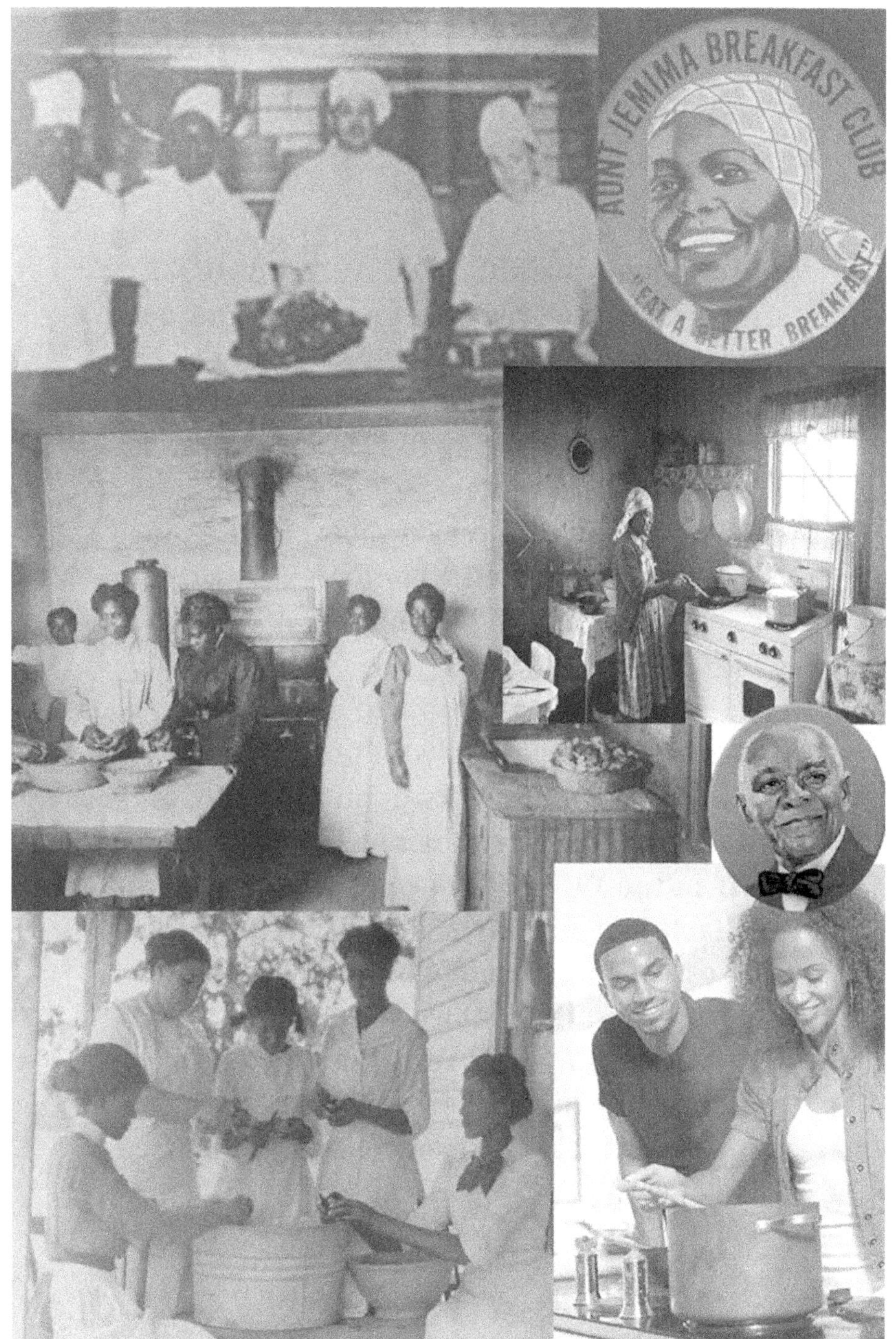
AUNT JEMIMA BREAKFAST CLUB
"EAT A BETTER BREAKFAST"

Photo Page 6
Hair Styles

Through out the history of America, Black American have created a variety of unique hair styles influence by their African culture shown here. Top left Joseph Erwin Kyles, authors father wearing the Ivy League style from 1946. Top center Author Sirron Kyles, shown wearing the very popular at the time Jerri Curl, 1970. Left Elbenia Kyles, 1955, wearing a White high fashion look created using the Hot Flat Iron.

 Braids have been a staple of African hair styles for centuries and still popular today shown here. In attempts to mimic white hair, many black men use chemicals to straighten their in the 19th & 20th century. A variety of Black hair products like TCB's Afro Sheen & Posner's Bergamot Conditioners and others maintain the Afro styles. In the 1970 Reggae artist made Dread Locks popular and are still worn today by many male and females which originated in Africa.

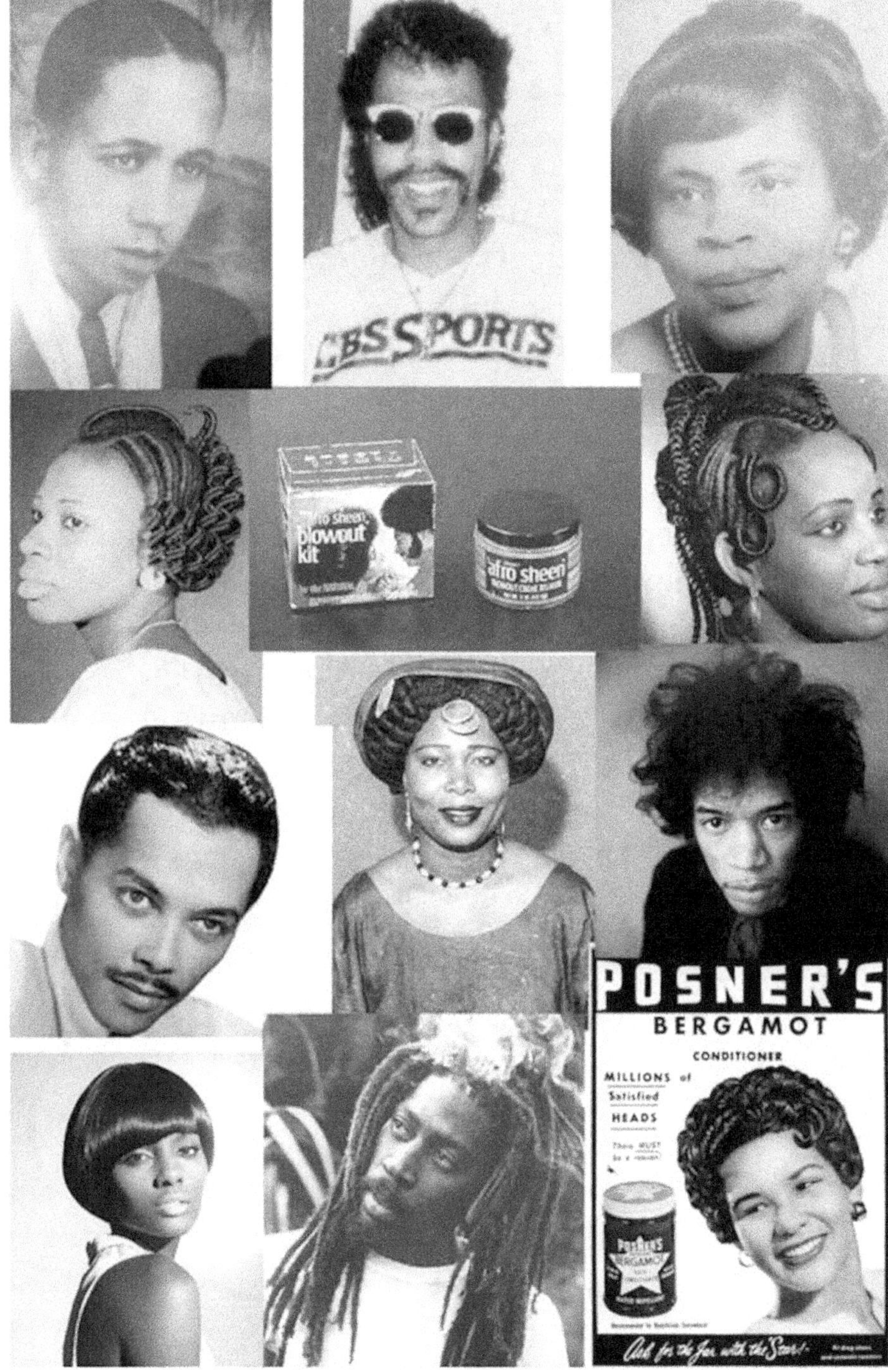
CBS SPORTS
afro sheen
blowout kit
afro sheen
POSNER'S
BERGAMOT
CONDITIONER
MILLIONS of
Satisfied
HEADS
There MUST
be a reason
POSNER'S
BERGAMOT
Ask for the Jar with the Star

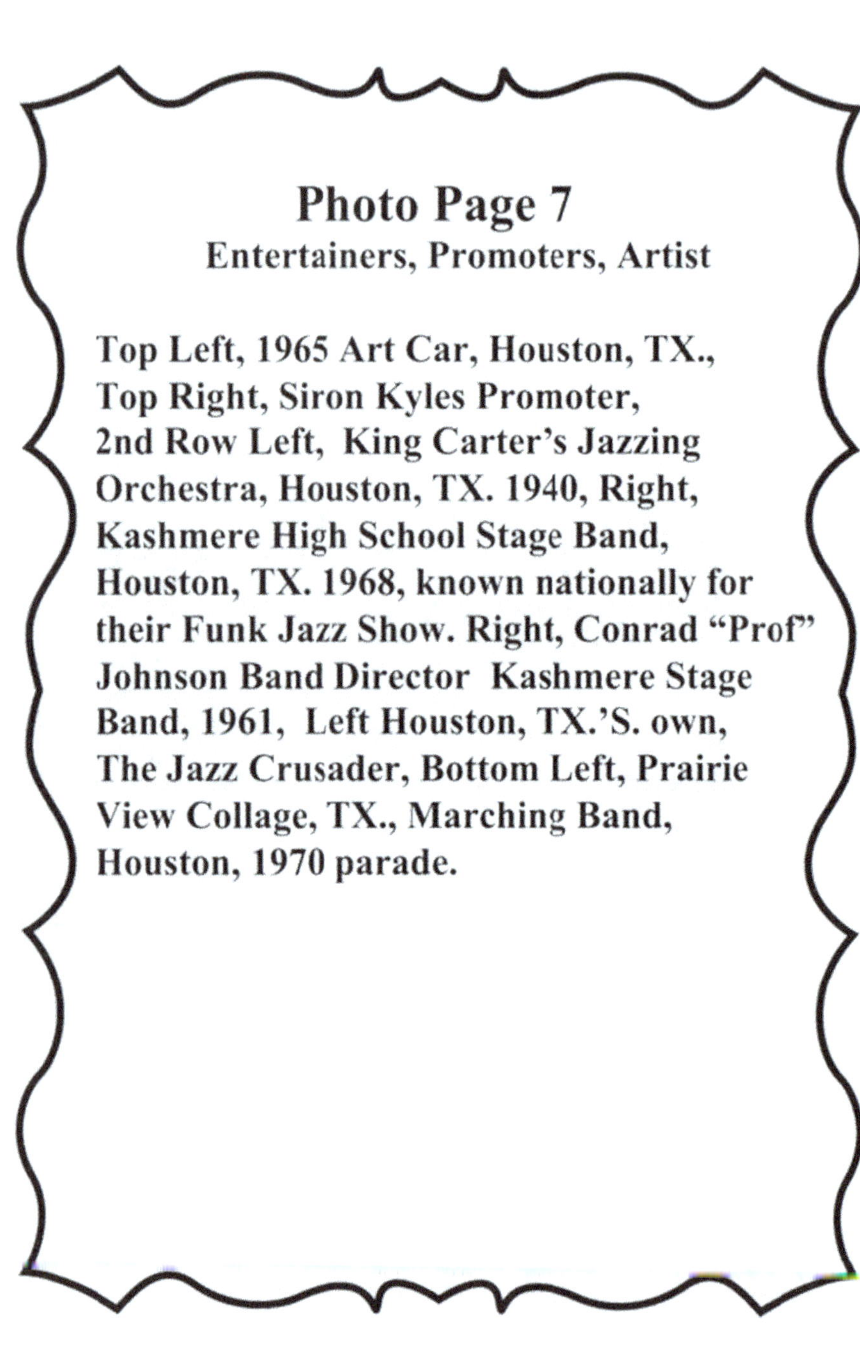

Photo Page 7
Entertainers, Promoters, Artist

Top Left, 1965 Art Car, Houston, TX.,
Top Right, Siron Kyles Promoter,
2nd Row Left, King Carter's Jazzing
Orchestra, Houston, TX. 1940, Right,
Kashmere High School Stage Band,
Houston, TX. 1968, known nationally for
their Funk Jazz Show. Right, Conrad "Prof"
Johnson Band Director Kashmere Stage
Band, 1961, Left Houston, TX.'S. own,
The Jazz Crusader, Bottom Left, Prairie
View Collage, TX., Marching Band,
Houston, 1970 parade.

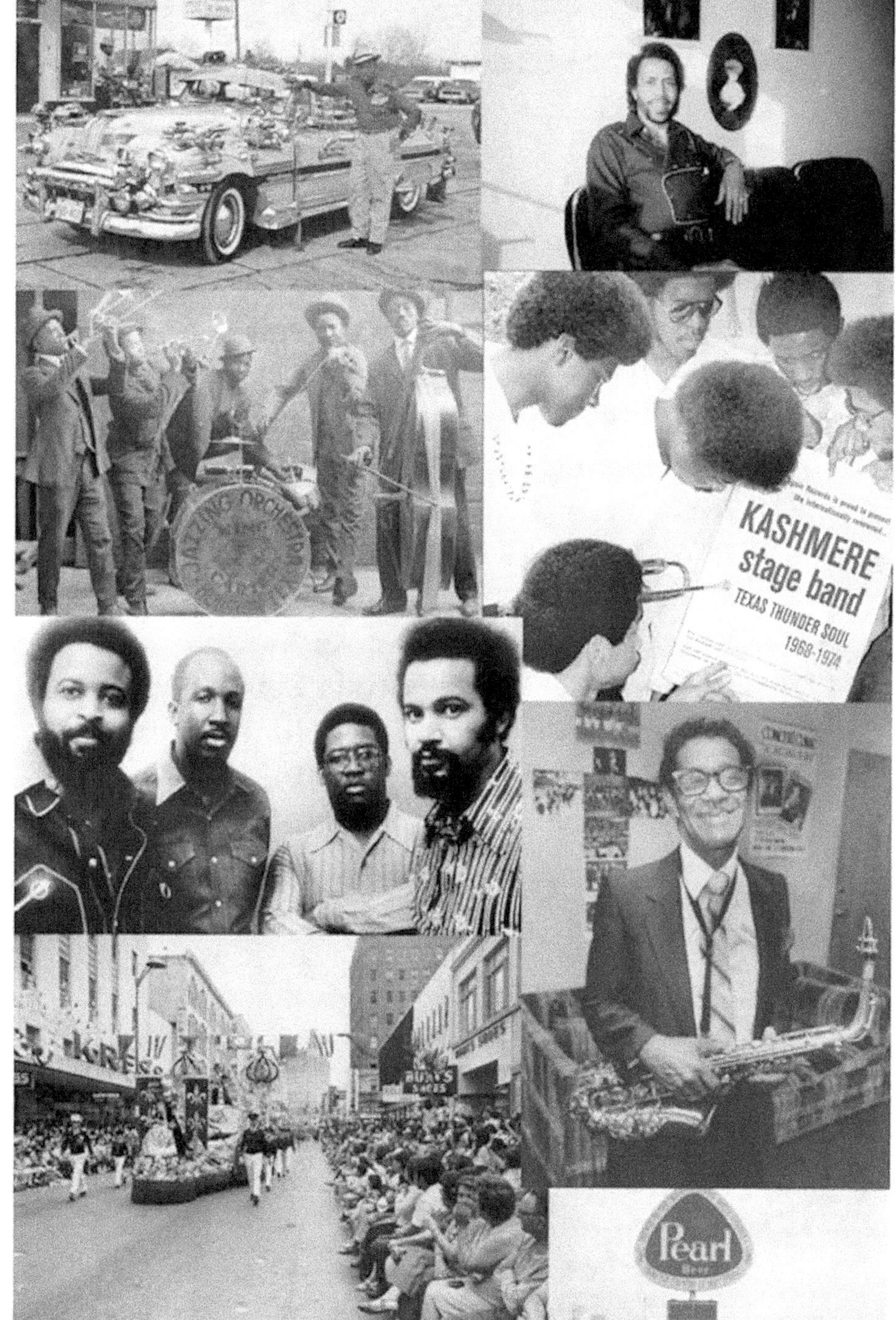
KASHMERE
stage band
TEXAS THUNDER SOUL
1968-1974
Pearl

Page 8
Performers of Color

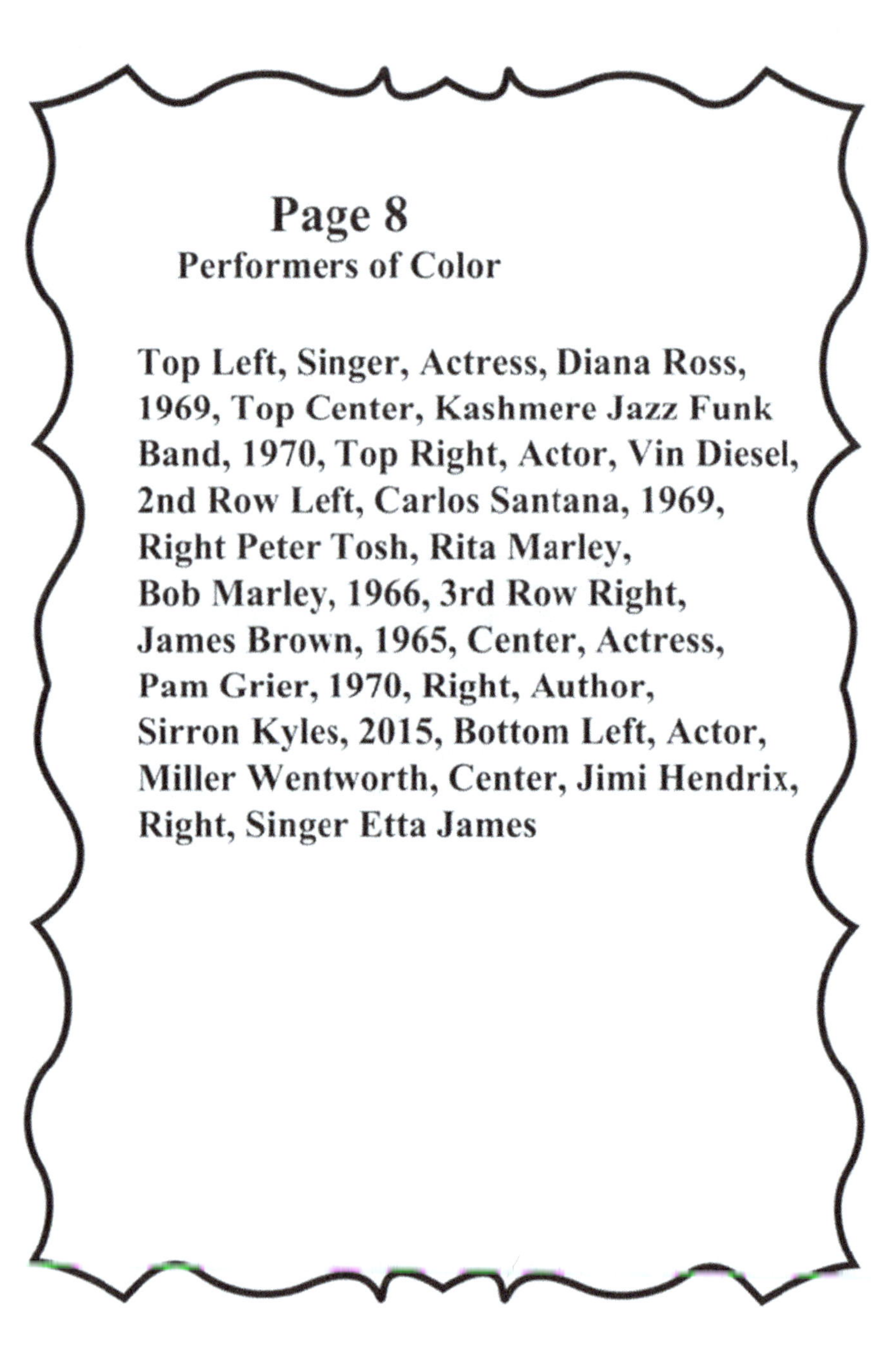

Top Left, Singer, Actress, Diana Ross,
1969, Top Center, Kashmere Jazz Funk
Band, 1970, Top Right, Actor, Vin Diesel,
2nd Row Left, Carlos Santana, 1969,
Right Peter Tosh, Rita Marley,
Bob Marley, 1966, 3rd Row Right,
James Brown, 1965, Center, Actress,
Pam Grier, 1970, Right, Author,
Sirron Kyles, 2015, Bottom Left, Actor,
Miller Wentworth, Center, Jimi Hendrix,
Right, Singer Etta James

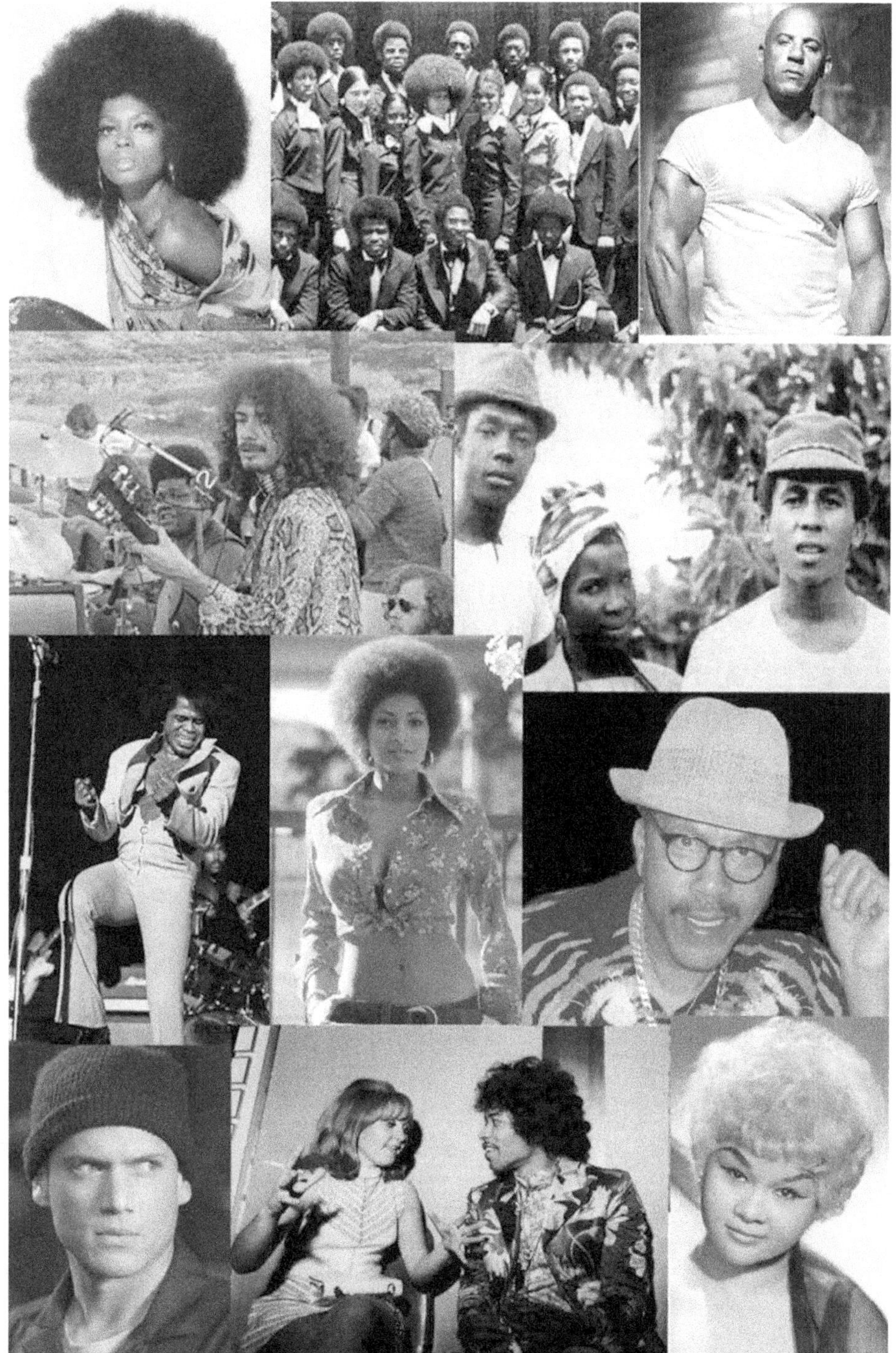

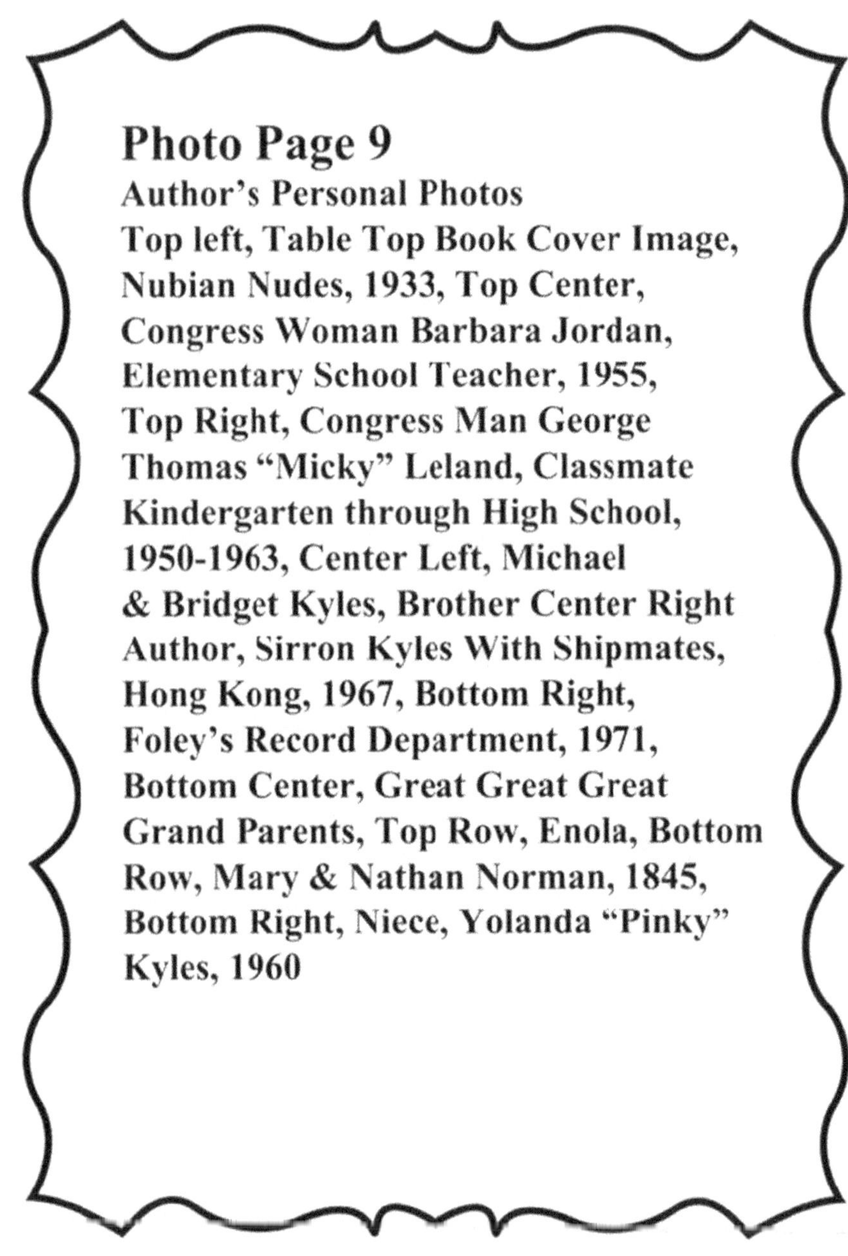

Photo Page 9
Author's Personal Photos
Top left, Table Top Book Cover Image,
Nubian Nudes, 1933, Top Center,
Congress Woman Barbara Jordan,
Elementary School Teacher, 1955,
Top Right, Congress Man George
Thomas "Micky" Leland, Classmate
Kindergarten through High School,
1950-1963, Center Left, Michael
& Bridget Kyles, Brother Center Right
Author, Sirron Kyles With Shipmates,
Hong Kong, 1967, Bottom Right,
Foley's Record Department, 1971,
Bottom Center, Great Great Great
Grand Parents, Top Row, Enola, Bottom
Row, Mary & Nathan Norman, 1845,
Bottom Right, Niece, Yolanda "Pinky"
Kyles, 1960

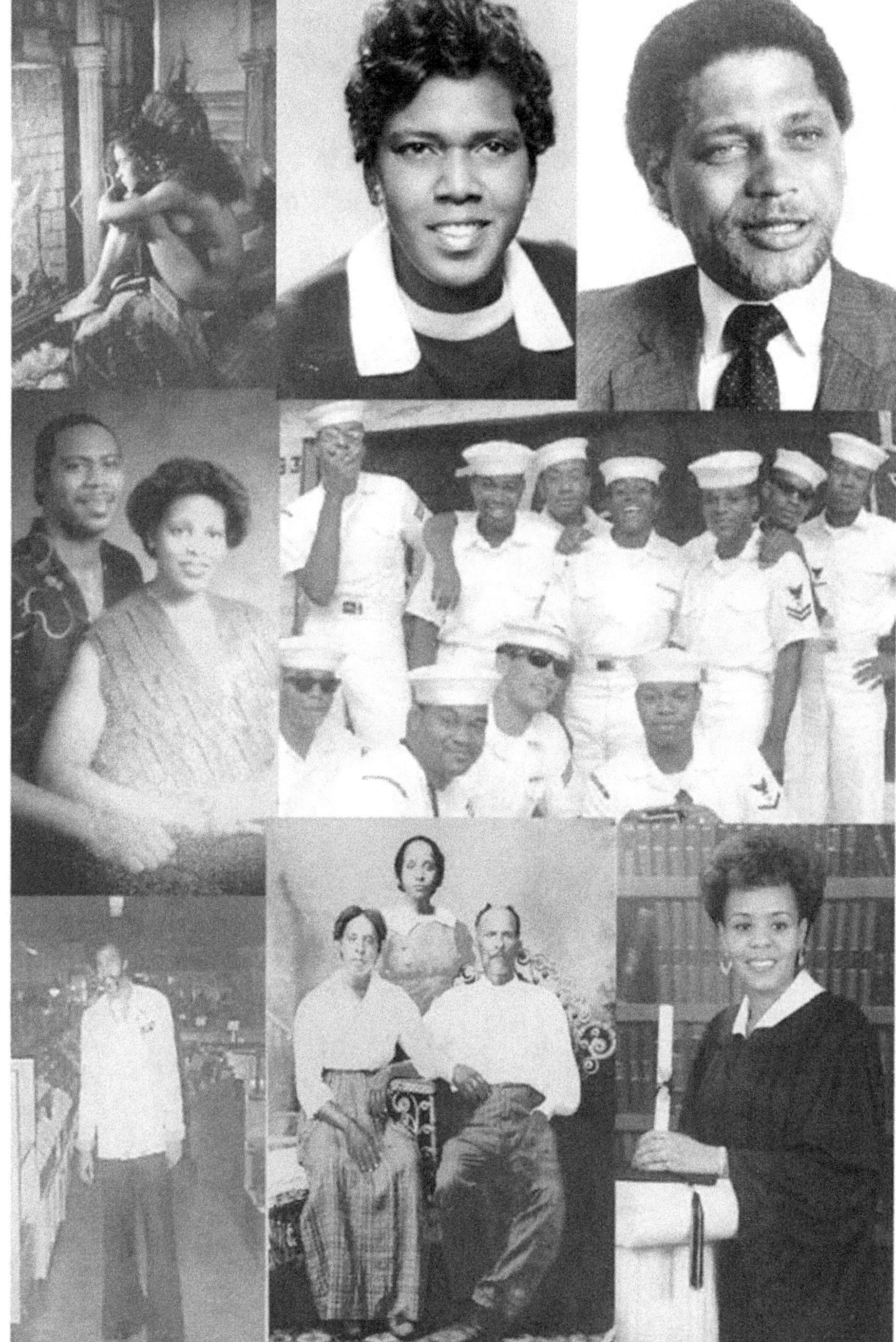

Photo Page 10
African American Fashions

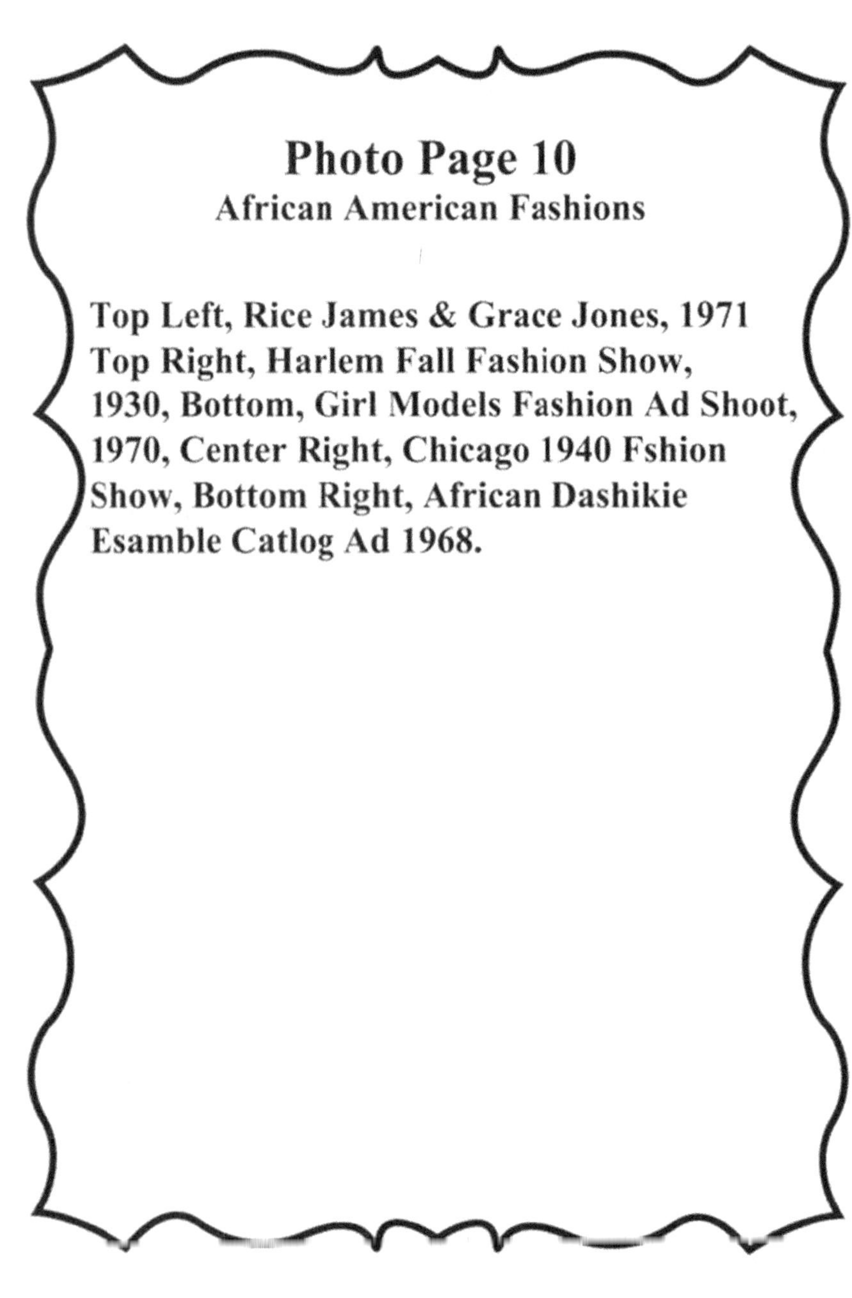

Top Left, Rice James & Grace Jones, 1971
Top Right, Harlem Fall Fashion Show,
1930, Bottom, Girl Models Fashion Ad Shoot,
1970, Center Right, Chicago 1940 Fshion
Show, Bottom Right, African Dashikie
Esamble Catlog Ad 1968.

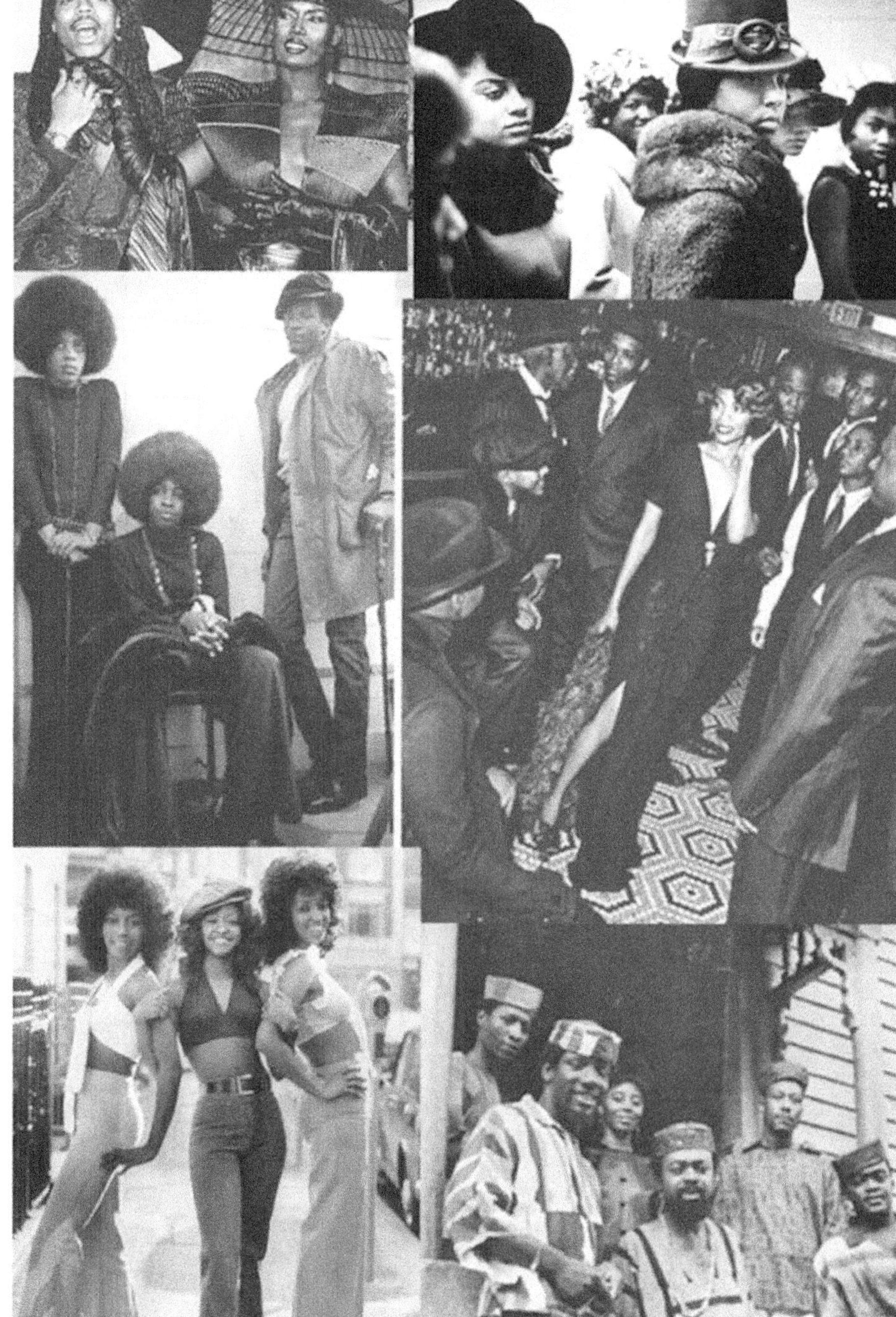

Photo Sources

Billy Roberts Photography
Dave Lovelace Photography
Wenn Photography
Graphicstock.com
Ed Kolenovsky Photography
State Archives Of Florida
New England Historical Society
H. Council Trenholm State Technical College archive in Alabama
Houston Post News Paper Archives
Houston Chronicle News Paper Archives
Vintage African American Photography
50ayear.com
Americanyawp.com
Logsoku.com
Africanamericanhistory.co